Artificial General Intelligence
A New Approach

Francis R. Belch

DEDICATION

To my wife Anne, my daughters Judith and Isabel, and my
son Alexander.

Table of Contents

ACKNOWLEDGMENTS

I must acknowledge the invaluable contribution of my research assistant Beatrice (Bebe) Webster.

INTRODUCTION

This book is all about a wholly new and revolutionary approach to the theory and implementation of Artificial General Intelligence (AGI) which was once called Strong Artificial Intelligence (AI). That is the sort of AI that can engage in a conversation with you in a natural language e.g., English, that can understand what you say, that can build a mental model from what you say, that can use that mental model, to answer your comprehension questions, to carry out logic and computation at your request, to form deductions, to detect omissions and inconsistencies, and to proactively remedy these. In fact, can interact with you in a very similar way to another intelligent person. You will perhaps recognise that this closely follows Alan Turing's recipe for AI (Cryan, Shatil, & Mayblin, Turing's recipe for AI, 2013). In fact, this is the functionality which is reflected in the title of this book; this is *Artificial General Intelligence*.

But let's warn you at this point, that some of the previous characteristics are shared by the frequently encountered chatbot, with which you may be familiar. But you will very soon see, we hope, that technology based on the new theory described here is far, far removed from any chatbot you have ever come across. This represents a totally original approach. Importantly, it avoids use of the neural network technique employed by the more complex chatbots, and by other applications such as vehicle number plate or handwriting recognition. The stochastic nature of neural networks results in opacity, that is producing answers that even their conceivers and implementers do not really understand. We promise that following the reading of this book you will find a system based on its theories to be totally comprehensible and transparent. The AI software demonstrator which you will encounter at the conclusion of this book, is not, and never has been, in communication with the web, and does not need to be, in order to function. Significantly, it does not require any form of training, which is characteristic of neural networks. This important fact implies that this technology is far more about finding new solutions to new problems, rather than searching the web for existing solutions to existing ones. Again, in sharp contrast to the neural network approach, the demonstrator requires very modest computational and memory resources and will run on pretty well any laptop or tablet supporting Windows®.

We are shortly going to begin an exciting voyage of discovery by looking, in *Part I* of this book, at the semantic information contained in that fundamental component of human communication, that short, formally, or informally structured succession of words we call a sentence. It may not be initially obvious where we are going with this in *Part I*, but we are eventually going to show, especially in *Part II*, that by analysing the informational content of individual sentences we can establish a method of melding information from a succession or group of sentences to arrive at a so-called mental model, sometimes referred to as an ontology.

We are going to discover common properties shared by all sentences irrespective of their construction. In fact, we are going to suggest in this discourse that it is impossible for the human mind to construct an intelligible sentence that does not accord with these properties.

We warn that you are unlikely to encounter the method of sentence semantic analysis we employ in *Part I* of this book in any learned volume, paper, or dissertation in the field of linguistics. In fact, the only method of analysis which even comes close, occurs in a text referred to as the *Port-Royal Grammar* which was published in 1660 by the Catholic theologians and logicians *Antoine Arnauld* and *Claude Lancelot*, who were members of the so-called *Messieurs de Port Royal* (Arnauld & Lancelot, 1753 translation). However, to allay your fears, we think that you will find that you do not need any specialist linguistic knowledge whatsoever to follow the arguments that we are shortly going to put to you. This book is really quite an easy read, we promise.

As well as well as beginning to provide an avenue to the implementation of general or strong AI, we show that there are profound philosophical implications stemming from this method of sentence analysis, which, we suggest may give clues to the origins and evolution of human language. They may also point to human language semantic universals, that is, properties and meanings shared in common with, and underlying all human languages in the world.

In *Part II* we show that, as previously mentioned, employment of the methods of sentence semantic analysis described in *Part I*, facilitates melding information from a succession or group of sentences associated with a dialogue or discourse, to build a special type of software-based mental model reflecting this same information. We show in *Part II* how it is possible to subsequently use this mental model to answer comprehension queries, perform logical deductions and computation and to generally begin to replicate our own thought and reasoning processes and responses. We suggest that by the end of *Part II* you may start to have the beginnings of an inkling that an AI system based on these principles might actually be feasible.

Again, we show that as well as providing an avenue to general of strong AI, the philosophical implications stemming from this type of mental model may challenge the conventional Aristotelian views of logic and reasoning (Cryan, Shatil, & Mayblin, The Syllogism, 2013), and may also provide novel insights into Set Theory (Cantor, 1895), perhaps even questioning its use as a fundamental basis for mathematics (Whitehead & Russell, 2019).

In *Part III* we try to address some significant issues associated with AGI technology. Are we assured that results from its use are always valid, and are we able to demonstrate or prove this? Does it pose any threat to human society associated with the possible autonomous appearance of super intelligence? Does this revolutionary theory in any way diminish the stature of historical literary works. All these and associated matters receive our attention.

In *Part IV* we describe the philosophy behind the conversational AI software demonstrator *AI Dialog*. This demonstrator, based on the theory of *Part I* and *Part II*, is able to comprehend a set of plain English sentences comprising a dialogue or discourse, expressed in either spoken or textual form, and to respond in spoken or textual plain English, to plain English queries testing this comprehension. It is also capable of carrying out reasoning, and the making of deductions from dialogue topics. Here is a very, very short example of functionality. The normal font shows our input and the italicised font the *AI Dialog* demonstrator's responses.

- A lady has two Siamese cats, three Burmese cats and a nervous budgie.
- *Right, I understand.*
- Each Siamese cat has two biscuits and three toys.
- *OK, got it.*

• Each Burmese cat has three more biscuits and two more toys.
• *Right, I understand.*
• The budgie has two more toys.
• *OK, got it.*
• Count each lady, each cat, each toy, each biscuit, and each budgie.
• *There is just one lady, five cats, 14 toys, 13 biscuits and one budgie.*

Part IV explains that one reason the *AI Dialog* software demonstrator has been developed is to explore the validity of the new sentence analysis concept and the use of software mental models or ontologies based on this concept; to obtain experimental proof of the concept, in fact. Another reason is to explore the analysis as a path, as previously mentioned, to advanced general or strong AI that can comprehend things, in exactly the same way we do ourselves.

In *Part IV* we show that the *AI Dialog* software demonstrator only scratches the surface potential of the technology that the book describes, and we briefly outline the exciting possible future developments of this software. We also discuss what we may learn of human mind and brain operation from the operation of this demonstrator, and the topics described earlier in *Parts I* and *II*.

In the penultimate *Appendix A* of this book, we tell you where you can get a freely available download of this software demonstrator, and describe its features and facilities. The demonstrator will run on most *Windows 10®* PCs and laptops and some tablets, using microphone and/or keyboard, speech, or textual input, and gives you the opportunity if you so wish, to personally explore these exciting topics for yourself.

INTRODUCTION

(This page is intentionally blank)

PART I

SENTENCE ANALYSIS

Let's begin with a really radical and novel claim in English language linguistic semantics, and in particular that part associated with individual sentence meaning.

MOST English sentences, with some to be explained exceptions, may be reduced ENTIRELY to just a series of simple:

   • *X is Y* and *X has Y* expressions

where X and Y are mostly single words, but occasionally phrases, from the sentence concerned.

We are going to show that in practice, it does not really matter:

   • how complex the sentence is
   • what its clause structure is
   • what parts of speech it employs,
   • what verbs and what tenses it uses

It can STILL be reduced to just a series of simple *is* and *has* or *is-has* expressions.

You may find this difficult to accept at first.

You may even find the concept totally outrageous.

Surely every sentence in the plays of Shakespeare, the novels of Chaucer, Dickens, and Austen, and the poems of Blake, Byron, and Coleridge cannot be reduced to just a series of *is-has* expressions? Well, we ask you to please be patient and continue to read, whilst we try to convince you that this really is the case.

Later in the book we will demonstrate that we can extend the principles described here to the building of a mental model from a group or succession of sentences constituting a dialogue. Much later we will show that this model can be used in a computer software application to demonstrate a general or strong AI system.

If you find the sentence analysis arguments put here convincing – and of course you may decide otherwise - we suggest later that they give clues to:

- The inner meanings of *to be* and *to have*
- The real nature of verbs
- How our minds work and how we think and reason
- The origins of human language
- A path to the principal topic of this book:
  - *Artificial General Intelligence* or Strong Artificial Intelligence

So, let's begin. We are going to start with very simple sentences and then progressively increase their complexity, showing how most major parts of speech can analysed and fitted into the concept, and where and why exceptions exist, and how these can be dealt with using extensions to the basic concept.

But keep that mental seat belt securely fastened, we are in for a really exciting ride.

Sentences into is-has expressions

Consider the example sentence, illustrated in the figure following:

- *The bright red balloon has a long string with a knot*

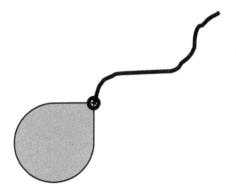

We hope you'll agree we can represent this sentence with short expressions like this:

- *balloon is red*
- *red is bright*
- *balloon has string*
- *string is long*
- *string has knot*

Each expression is of the form:

- *X is Y* or *X has Y*

So, we have:

• *balloon is red*	(X is Y)
• *red is bright*	(X is Y)
• *balloon has string*	(X has Y)
• *string is long*	(X is Y)
• *string has knot*	(X has Y)

At this point you may be feeling some disquiet. In the example the word *red* is an adjective. In classical syntax analysis, adjectives are always used to describe nouns, such as *balloon*. But *bright* could be regarded as an adverb. Again, in classical analysis adverbs are always used to describe either adjectives, *red* in the example, or other adverbs or verbs. But as you can see, the meaning of *is* is sufficiently broad to work with a whole range of word pair types and we do not need to worry about differences between adjectives and adverbs.

Much later in this book we are going to try to delve into the meanings of *is* and *has*.

Active *has* and passive *of*
Now we need to take a brief detour.

We hope you will agree that the following two expressions are related

- *balloon has string*
- *string of balloon*

both imply *the balloon has a string*.

In the second expression the subject *balloon* and object *string* change places and *has* is replaced by *of*.

So, we suggest that in many situations, although certainly not all, *of* behaves as a sort of inverse of *has*.

So, in these situations we may say:

- *X has Y*   implies *Y of X*
  - or:
- *Y of X*   implies *X has Y*

We will make use of these relations in many of the examples that follow, to clarify the logic we are using.

We note that *of* is sometimes used as a passive relative of *is*, as in *the balloon is red* and *the red of the balloon*. Also, we can relate *is* to *has* by saying, for example *the balloon has redness*. But in practice in what follows we are not going to make use of either of these relations.

Sentence conversion examples

You may be thinking at this point, that's all very well for a very simple example sentence, of the type previously chosen, but what happens if we move to more complex sentences.

To begin to answer that, let's move to a slightly more complex example sentence. Consider the sentence, illustrated in the figure following:

- *the train is inside the station*

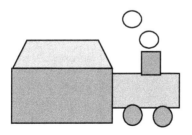

Let's begin to analyse this sentence.

We can make a start with an *is* expression by saying:

- *train is inside*

We don't really need to enquire *inside* what at present, the concept can stand on its own. The *train* is *inside* something unspecified.

Now consider … *inside the station* and ignore the previous. At this point we seem to get stuck don't we?

Or perhaps not.

If we think about it, we can imagine that the *station* has a *booking-hall* and a *platform*, which we could characterise by the *has* expressions like this:

- *station has booking-hall*
      and
- *station has platform*

and so on, just as we earlier had the *balloon* having a *string*. So, is it too outrageous to suggest then that the *station* can have an *inside*, reflected in the expression:

- *station has inside*

If we can accept this, we can now complete the analysis and say:

- *train is inside*
- *station has inside*

analysing the sentence as promised, with an *is* expression and a *has* expression. But, using the previously discussed *has/of* relation we can also say:

- *station has inside*
      implies
- *inside of station*

which sounds rather more familiar. You may, in fact sometimes hear a person use the expression the *train is inside of the station*.

It may be pedantic at this point, but we need to emphasise that with the expressions:

- *train is inside*
      and
- *station has inside*

the *inside* is actually the same *inside* in both expressions.

This is not indicated by the previous expressions alone, but we can bring out and clarify this relationship by using a so-called semantic network, as shown in the diagram following:

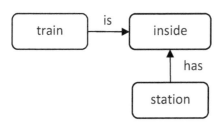

We will describe semantic networks in greater detail later, but briefly for now, in the diagram, the *train*, the *station* and the *inside* are so-called nodes (in some texts referred to a vertices) and the *is* and *has* relationships are so-called directed edges. They are directed because they have arrows leading from a source node to a destination node (Lehman, 1992).

The semantic network shows clearly that the common *inside* is shared by the *train* and the *station*.

Here are two more example sentences illustrated in the figure following:

- *the road is beside the station*
- *the station is beside the road*

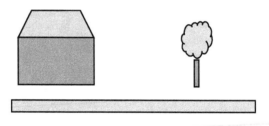

We can analyse these in a similar way:

- *the road is beside the station*
    - *road is beside*
    - *station has beside (beside of station)*
- *the station is beside the road*
    - *station is beside*
    - *road has beside (beside of road)*

Considering these examples in detail.

Very significantly, the word *beside* in the top two, that is:

- *road is beside*
- *station has beside*

actually, differs from *beside* in the lower two:

- *station is beside*
- *road has beside*

If you think about it, the reason for this is because there may be other things *beside* the *road*, which are not *beside* the *station*.

Again, these relationships are brought out much more clearly using a semantic network shown following:

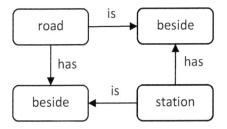

This shows the *beside* associated with the road and the separate *beside* associated with the station.

Here are two more example sentences, illustrated in the figure following:

- *the plane is above the station*
- *the station is below the plane*

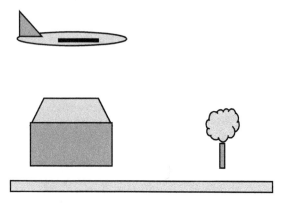

Similarly, with these, the analysis is as follows:

- *the plane is above the station*
  - *plane is above*
  - *station has above*
- *the station is below the plane*
  - *station is below*
  - *plane has below*

Note, with these and the earlier sentences, how *inside, beside, above* and *below* have started to become properties of the *station, road,* and *plane* – something each *has,* a sort of property of each. So, the *station* has *inside, beside,* and *above* properties, the *road* has a *beside* property, and the *plane* has a *below* property. These properties tend to be associated with solid objects. Something like a *gas,* say, would only have the *inside* property, not the others. We are going to return to this concept later.

The corresponding semantic network for the previous example is again shown following:

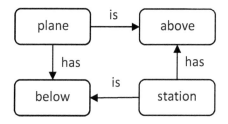

General verbs

So far, we have considered only the present tense, third person singular of verbs *to be* and *to have*, that is, *is* and *has*. Is it possible to generalise the previous concepts to other verbs?

Consider the sentence, illustrated in the figure following:

- *Jack climbs up the hill.*

This looks rather daunting initially, perhaps, to convert into an *is-has* representation. In particular, the verb *climbs*, present tense, third person singular of the verb *to climb*, initially does not appear conducive to this type of analysis.

So how on earth are we going to manage it?

Let's begin by converting the verb *climbs* to the present participle *is climbing*, so we now get:

  • *Jack is climbing up the hill*

But wait, we can hear you say, doesn't *Jack climbs* differ slightly in meaning from *Jack is climbing*?

This is true, *Jack climbs* is case perfect, with some implication the *climbing* activity is over and done with, although quite recently.

Jack *is climbing* is case imperfect, with some implication the *climbing* activity continues.

We suggest in practice the sentence would tend to occur as part of a sequence of events, and how we would interpret the sentence would depend on the situation. So, in common parlance we perhaps do not need make a big deal out of the difference in meaning between *Jack climbs* and *Jack is climbing*. However, much later on, in *Part II* of this book in the section *Sequences of events*, we will show how we can handle any case differences rather more precisely.

For now, in the interests of simplicity, we are simply going to pass over it.

So, our analysis of

  • *Jack is climbing up the hill*

begins with:

- *Jack is climbing*
- *climbing is up*

In a similar way to the previous example of *the train is inside the station* we may consider the first part *Jack is climbing* as an assertion Jack is a member of the set of people or things doing *climbing,* we do not need as yet to question as yet what *Jack* is *climbing.*

The *climbing is up* is straightforward, we have the adverb *up* qualifying the participle *climbing,* using an *is* expression.

This then leaves us with the problem of *climbing (up) the hill.*

Now, in a similar way to the earlier *station* example, the *hill* may be viewed as having various features or properties, for example, *trees* or *grass,* reflected in *the hill has trees* or *the hill has grass.*

Similarly, with imagination, we may view *climbing* also as a feature or property of the *hill,* reflected in *the hill has climbing.*

As with the *train/station* example, we can use the *has/of* transformation and instead of saying *the hill has climbing* we could say *the climbing of the hill,* which sounds more familiar.

However, there are some semantic issues with the *has/of* transformation when used with a participle, as just here with *climbing,* which we are going to defer for a paragraph or two, in order to maintain the momentum of our arguments.

So finally, we have:

• *Jack is climbing up the hill*

- *Jack is climbing*
- *climbing is up*
- *hill has climbing*

You may ask why *climbing* is not a property of *Jack* instead of, or as well as the *hill*, after all *Jack* apparently has a *climbing* capability. We suggest that although *Jack* is capable of *climbing*, however much he may desire to *climb*, he is not able to *climb*, unless a *climbing* environment, that is, something to *climb*, is provided by something else, that is, the *hill*. We reflect the *hill* providing this environment, facilitating Jack to perform the action of *climbing*. You may recognise this as not being too different from the earlier example of a *station* having an *inside*, a *beside* and an *above*.

Let's explore this further. Suppose *Jack* was in outer space, away from any celestial or manufactured body, as shown in the figure following. Could *Jack* do any *climbing*?

We suggest not. *Jack* needs something to *climb* before he can *climb*.

In our case that something is the *hill*. The *climbing* is just as much a property of the *hill*, as it is of *Jack*. If the *hill* is not there, then *climbing* is not possible. If the *hill* is there then *climbing* becomes possible.

There has to be a cooperative arrangement between the hill providing the environment for *climbing* to be possible, and *Jack* actually doing the *climbing*. Another analogy is a *peg* in a *hole* one. For a *peg* to be present in a *hole*, the *hole* must be provided and then the *peg*. If either is absent then a *peg* in a *hole* is not possible.

Finally, in the figure following, we have the semantic network representation of the analysis of *Jack is climbing up the hill*.

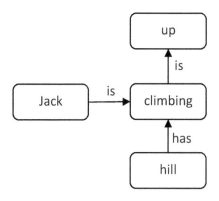

The network brings out again that the *climbing* which appears in all three of the earlier *is-has* expressions is actually the same *climbing*.

Semantic issues surrounding participles

Let's now pause to discuss some of the previously deferred semantic issues surrounding participles such as *climbing*.

An initial issue is that the phrase *grass of hill* implies *hill has grass* because *grass* is a noun. But *climbing of hill* could imply either, *the act of climbing* with *climbing* interpreted as a verb's participle, or a noun as in, for example, *the hill's climbing is good*.

But a much more significant further aspect that needs consideration is that *grass* seems to be a passive property of a *hill*, whilst *climbing* appears to be an active property i.e. it is something that you can *do* to the *hill*. You could describe this as an operable property.

Let's just step back a little and consider our own mental perceptions. There is information that we passively receive from the world. If we were a computer, which in some respects perhaps we are, we would term this information input information or our inputs. But we suggest that there are other things that we cannot find out about unless we take some action ourselves. For example, we may not know if something is heavy or light unless we grab hold of it and test its weight. These aspects of objects are associated with our outputs; we have to actively do something in order to find out about something.

So, let's define operable properties as things it is possible for us to do to objects. For example Jack can *climb* a *hill* but he cannot *eat* it. Jack can *eat* an *apple* but he cannot *drink* it, and so on. For any object of our perception we can list its operable properties. Later on in *Part II* there is a section *Definitions, instances and meanings* we discuss definitions. Whilst deferring a detailed discussion at this juncture, we can define things as having various operable properties e.g., *hill has climbing* or *apple has eating* and so on.

In respect of operable properties you might argue for *Jack does climbing* rather than *Jack is climbing* for the *climbing* property. Support also for this view is that *to do* is the third auxiliary verb that English has, along with *to be* and *to have*.

The first argument we mount against this is that we can use i*s-has* expressions themselves to qualify *climbing* e.g. *climbing is up*. Secondly, we say *climbing of the hill* as well as *grass of the hill*, i.e., we do not use a different inverse *has* expression. Thirdly, we can keep our semantic expressions i.e., semantic network edge labels, to a minimum by confining ourselves to just *is* and *has*.

We suggest that effectively if we use *is* followed by a participle, i.e., generally by a word ending with *ing,* we are causing some shift in the meaning of *is*. Later in this book again in the section entitled *Definitions, instances, and meanings* we are going to see how the meaning of *is* changed when we follow it by an indefinite article e.g. *a* as in *Jack is a farmer*. So, we suggest that in a way *is* may be regarded is a sort of portmanteau concept or semantic operator.

Right at the start of this discourse we claimed that all English sentences could be analysed into *is* and *has* expressions. Here we are starting to see that such expressions do not always represent exactly the same semantics even though the relational verb remains the same. Later, we will see that this does not generally affect their utility in the formation of our mental models.

So, the final litmus test is, does the *is climbing* representation, and similar participles representing operable properties, lead to usable technology, to which the answer would appear to be in the affirmative. Acknowledging this we will decide to confine ourselves to the use of *is* and *has* to handle what we have termed operable properties as well as what we have termed passive properties in everything that follows.

We are going to say some further things about expressions such as *Jack is climbing,* and *hill has climbing* in a later section entitled *The real nature of verbs.* We will suggest then that verbs are more subtle and complex entities than we perhaps appreciate.

We should also note in connection with the syntax of participles occurring in sentences, words qualifying the participle tend to occur after it e.g., we say *climbing up* rather than *up climbing.* We can contrast this with words qualifying nouns e.g., we say *red balloon* rather than *balloon red.* Although we call words qualifying participles *adverbs* and words qualifying nouns *adjectives*, we suggest they do a similar job. We will see later in the mental model that in fact we make very little distinction between them.

Multiple instances and absence of target

There may be multiple instances of *climbing* associated with the same *hill.* For example, we may have *Jack climbs up the hill* as illustrated in the previous figure, and *Jill climbs down the hill* as shown following. But even if the *up* and *down* qualifiers were absent, we would still have separate instances of *climbing* associated with *Jack* and *Jill,* respectively.

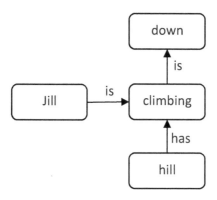

One final point is that *climbing* could occur in a sentence without mention of anything to *climb* e.g., just *Jack is climbing* without any target. Here, we suggest that we mentally assume that he is *climbing* something and accept the fact that we are lacking information about what exactly.

Some further examples

Consider the sentence *Jack likes Jill.*

Again, we change the verb *likes* to the present participle *is liking* so we have *Jack is liking Jill.* The phrase *Jack is liking* which is reflected in the semantic network *A* in the figure following, shows *Jack* being a member of a *liking* set, that is, a set of people who are *liking* something. Again, if *Jack* was on his own in the universe, it would not be possible for Jack to *like* anything. *Jill* provides the *liking* environment, reflected in the semantic network *B*. We then combine the two networks as shown in *C*. We note that by the *has/of* transformation *Jill has liking* may also be expressed as *the liking of Jill*.

Let's emphasise that this does not mean *Jill* necessarily *likes Jack*; *Jill* is just providing the environment for *Jack* to do his *liking*. If we wish to show the reciprocity reflected in the further sentence *Jill likes Jack,* then we add a *liking* environment to *Jack* and make *Jill* a member of another *liking* set, as shown in *D*.

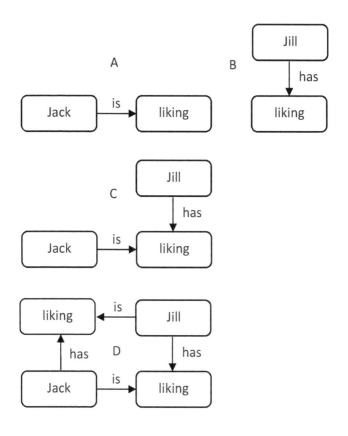

Here is a yet more challenging example, *Jack likes to tease Jill.*

Here we can convert the verb *likes* into the participle *is liking*

as before. The phrase *to tease* poses some challenges. We suggest that it is valid to convert *to tease* into *the teasing of.* If you are happy with this conversion, then it provides us with a mechanism for converting the frequently occurring phrase *to ... do something* in sentences. This is one of the many syntactic abbreviations that have developed in English. Another interesting example is the word *for* which we will deal with in a while. Accepting the suggested conversion allows us to proceed further and gives us:

> • *Jack is liking the teasing of Jill.*

We can then analyse this as follows:

> • *Jack is liking the teasing of Jill.*
>   - *Jack is liking*
>   - *teasing has liking (liking of teasing)*
>   - *Jill has teasing (teasing of Jill)*

Note that, by the *has/of* transformation, in the above, *teasing has liking* is the same as *liking of teasing*, and *Jill has teasing* is the same as *teasing of Jill.*

Yet again, in each expression, the *liking* is the same *liking* and the *teasing* the same *teasing*, so the *teasing* remains as done by *Jack* and not by somebody else.

Again, we suggest, as with the *Jack climbing up the hill* example, that if *Jill* is not present, then the *teasing* would not be possible, so the *teasing* is a property of *Jill.* In similar way, if the *teasing* is not present, then the *liking of teasing* is not possible, so the *liking* is a property of the *teasing*.

Finally, in the figure following, we have the semantic network representation of the previous sentence analysis.

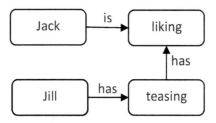

Verb tenses other than the present

So far, we've just dealt with verbs in the present tense. So, can we accommodate verbs in other tenses? Before answering this question, we make two points.

The first point is, in English, if we describe something as happening in the past, future, or any other tense, we modify just the verbs, not any other parts of speech, that is not the nouns, adjectives, adverbs, or prepositions, and so on. But with the past tense and an example such as, *the boy swam the river,* this implies that the *boy* and the *river* are also in the past at the time that the *swimming* takes place, and not just the *swimming* itself. We suggest this applies to other tenses too; the verb drags anything associated with it into its own tense.

The second and more significant point is, that if we read a novel, the verbs we encounter whilst reading are usually in the past tense, for example, *Jack fetched the pail, Jack climbed the hill, Jack found the spring, Jack filled the pail* and so on. Occasionally novels are cast in the present tense, for example, *Jack fetches the pail, Jack climbs the hill, Jack finds the spring, Jack fills the pail.* In either case, as we read, in our minds, the action seems to occur at the very instant we read each sentence.

Even with an historical novel, where all the events described happened long ago, we suggest that as we read, in our minds, the action still seems to take place at the very instant we read each sentence. Our imagination takes us to that point in the past, just as though we had time-travelled there, and then after that everything seems to take place right now at the instant we read. This applies to any other tense we might encounter.

We therefore suggest that in any sentence we read, we can separate out the tense, and treat the action as if it were occurring right now in the present, since this appears to be what happens in our minds.

Past tense

Let's now examine the past tense by pitching one of the earlier sentences we encountered into this tense by saying:

> • *Jack climbed*
> instead of:
> • *Jack climbs*

This now gives us the past tense sentence:

> • *Jack climbed up the hill*

So, how can we handle this tense shift? Here is a method. We can do it by re-wording the sentence as follows:

> • *In the past, Jack climbs up the hill*

We think you will agree that the second part of the sentence i.e., *Jack climbs up the hill* is now in the present tense and is in fact the same as in one of the earlier examples. It can in fact now be analysed in exactly the same way as the earlier example. All we have to do is to flag the individual *is-has* expressions resulting from the analysis as occurring in the past. However, in practice, we do not do it like this:

> • *Jack climbed up the hill*
> > *- Jack was climbing*
> > *- climbing was up*
> > *- hill had climbing*

but, as we will expand upon later, we do it as shown following:

> • *Jack climbed up the hill*
> > *- (past)*
> > *- Jack is climbing*
> > *- climbing is up*
> > *- hill has climbing*

We do it this way, as we suggest, following the earlier discussion, it more closely aligns with the mental model we form in practice in our own minds.

In the semantic network representation of the analysis, shown following, we can enclose the whole of this semantic network in a *past* context to show that the *past* tense is applicable to it. In *Part II*, in the section *Contexts and network nodes* we are going to revisit this topic and explain exactly what a *context* is when employed in this way.

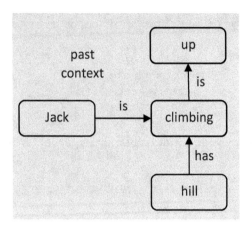

Future tense

Looking now at the future tense. If we pitch the earlier sentence into the future tense by saying:

> • *Jack will climb*
> instead of
> • *Jack climbs*

we get:

> • *Jack will climb up the hill*

We can tackle it in a similar way to the past tense, by rewording the sentence as:

> • *In the future, Jack climbs up the hill*

Which results in the analysis:

> • *In the future, Jack climbs up the hill*
>   *- (future)*

- *Jack is climbing*
- *climbing is up*
- *hill has climbing*

Again, in the semantic network representation of the analysis shown following, we now enclose the whole semantic network in a *future* context.

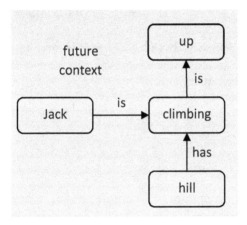

Mixed tenses

Let's look at another example, illustrated in the figure following:

- *The girl who won the race will get a prize*

Sometimes a sentence, as with this example, may contain a mixture of tenses. Here is an analysis of the example. Firstly, we re-word the sentence as:

> • *In the past, the girl is winning the race and, in the future, is getting a prize*

Then we analyse it as follows:

> • *In the past, the girl is winning the race and, in the future, is getting a prize*
>> - *(past)*
>> - *girl is winning*
>> - *race has winning (winning of race)*
>> - *(future)*
>> - *girl is getting*
>> - *prize has getting (getting of prize)*

Finally, in the figure following we have the semantic network representation of the analysis of the sentence. Note that in this case, *girl* exists in both the *past* and the *future* as indicated by the intersection of the *past* and *future* contexts.

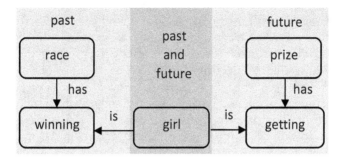

More complex tenses

Using the concept of contexts, we can accommodate more complex tenses, for example, the pluperfect, an example of which would be *when I arrived, the flight had left*. Here we have an event in the past i.e., *my arrival*, associated with an event even further in the past i.e., *the flight had left*. This would be represented as a past context having another past context nested within it, as shown in the semantic network following.

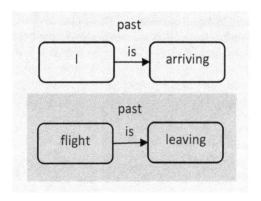

Adjective/adverb strings

Let's move on now from a consideration of verbs and their tenses, and have a look at another different topic, that of adjective/adverb strings. We are going to see that these are associated with *is*-type expressions. We have come across adjectives and adverbs earlier in the *balloon* example. English provides a sort of shorthand semantic support for these words, which subsequently result in *is*-type expressions. For example, in the phrase *the very large, dark red balloon* ... we put a string of words such as *very, large, dark* and *red,* which we call adjectives or adverbs, before another word such as *balloon* which we call a noun, as an abbreviation for the more verbose expressions *the balloon is red ...the red is dark ... the balloon is large ... the large is very* and so on. The semantic network for these, in which each adjective or adverb appears as a node, is shown in the figure following.

If the very same adjectives or adverbs appear in clauses instead, for example *the very* large *balloon that is dark red* ... we hope you will agree that the same semantic network is derived. We are going to say more about clauses shortly.

A note of caution however, words before nouns may be other nouns as in *control room.* Often such sequences are hyphenated as in *control-room,* but often they are not. The interpretation then differs, as discussed in the next section.

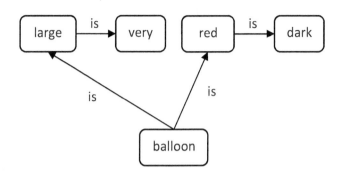

The very large, dark red balloon ...

or

The very large balloon that is dark red ...

Possessives and hyphens

In a similar way to adjectives or adverbs and *is*-type expressions, English provides some shorthand semantic support for the concept of ownership associated with *has*-type expressions. There are variations with *has*. In the *balloon* example, somebody or something may *have* the *balloon*, or the *balloon* may *have* something. Either may be handled using the possessive, for example, *the boy's balloon* representing *the boy has the balloon*, or *the balloon's string* representing *the balloon has the string*, shown in the semantic networks *A* and *B* following, respectively. You might argue that *boy's balloon* just implies ownership, not necessarily actual possession, but the corresponding phrase *boy has balloon* is just as imprecise.

Cases where the *boy, balloon,* or *string has* something and so on, may also be handled more verbosely by expressions such as *the balloon with the string* or *the string of the balloon* or in clauses such as *the balloon that has the string*. All of these examples lead to the same expression *the balloon has the string* shown in semantic network *B*.

A hyphen also may be used to infer possession, for example *the control-room* …, but there may be ambiguity here and we could argue for *the room that has control* … or *the room that control has* …. By convention, we generally plump for the former interpretation *the room has control* shown in semantic network *C*. If we want the other interpretation, we can always say *control's room*. A similar hyphenated expression is *apple-pie* implying *pie has apple*.

We have to be careful, because often hyphens are implied but are absent. For example in the phrase *in Xanadu did Kubla Khan a stately pleasure dome decree* you could optionally hyphenate *pleasure dome* because this is not a noun *dome* preceded by an adjective *pleasure*, meaning *dome is pleasure*, but a noun *dome* preceded by another noun *pleasure* meaning *dome has pleasure*. As mentioned earlier in the situation of adjective/adverb strings, we have to tread carefully and determine if the word in a sequence before a noun is an adjective or adverb or another noun, and interpret accordingly,

Deserving of special mention is the possessive used with a participle in, for example, *Jack's climbing*. This does not imply *Jack has climbing* but *Jack is climbing*. However, *mountain's climbing* in for example *the mountain's climbing is good* implies the *mountain has climbing*. So there are some challenging problems here depending on whether *climbing* is being interpreted as a verb's participle or a noun.

It is notable that although expressions such as *the string of the balloon* and *the balloon that has the string* have the same semantic network *B*, there is some additional information in each expression which is lost in the transformation. This issue of lost information is dealt with in much more detail later.

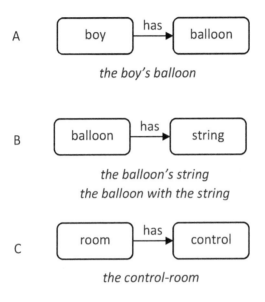

A

the boy's balloon

B

the balloon's string
the balloon with the string

C

the control-room

Sharing

A variant of possession uses the verb *sharing*. If we have *Jack and Jill each shares the pail*, this is represented as in the figure following. Rather more complex considerations apply here, and we will return to this topic in the later *Part IV The AI Dialog demonstrator*.

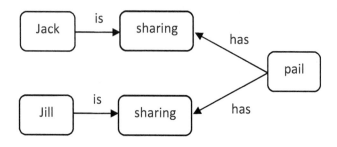

Prepositions

We have come across one or two prepositions already e.g., *inside, beside, above* and *below,* earlier in the *train, station, road,* and *plane* examples. Let's have a look at another preposition. If we say:

> • *Jack is buying a pail for Jill*

what does *for* mean exactly here?

This is the sort of preposition that we don't really think about in our English usage. We think we know what it means. But do we really? Generally, to do our *is-has* analyses we need to think carefully about issues like this, and then find some way to ascribe meaning to such prepositions in terms of *is-has*

expressions, and used in situations such as the one illustrated. We suggest in this particular case that:

> - *for Jill*
> means
> - *that Jill will have*

The sentence can then be analysed as:

> • *Jack is buying a pail for Jill*
>   - *(present) Jack is buying*
>   - *(present) pail has buying (buying of pail)*
>   - *(future) Jill has pail*

The semantic network is shown following. The act of *Jack buying the pail* is in the present, and the *pail* exists in the present and future. You can argue that *Jill* is both present and future too, which is not out of the question – it depends on whether *Jill* has been born at the time of *Jack is buying the pail*. The diagram shows the present and future contexts and the context overlap.

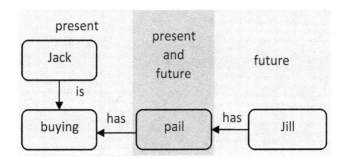

Attributing a meaning to a preposition such as *for* used in a particular way, illustrates the challenge posed by attributing meanings to prepositions in general in terms of *is* and *has* relationships.

Direct & indirect objects

Let's move on to a more complex sentence construct. The previous examples covered sentences with direct objects. We may in theory have *Jack climbs* with no object, reflected in *Jack is climbing* of the earlier example. We are going to discuss problems associated with this concept in the later section *The real nature of verbs*. But, conversely, we may have sentences with both direct and indirect objects (Seely, Indirect object, 2004), for example, *Jack gives the pail to Jill*. So, how do we analyse this type of sentence?

Let's address the example of *Jack gives the pail to Jill*.

Stepping back, we hope you will agree that this has a direct object *pail* and an indirect object *Jill*.

In our approach, we first change the sentence *Jack gives the pail to Jill* to

• *Jack is giving the pail to(wards) Jill*.

Then we consider the phrase *Jack is giving* as shown above and in the following semantic network *A*.

- *Jack is giving*

Then we consider *Jack is giving the pail*, which is like the earlier *Jack is climbing the hill.* By the previously discussed principles, the *pail* must be there for *Jack* to do any *giving*, so we have:

- *pail has giving (giving of pail)*

and reflected in semantic network *B*.

Then we consider *to Jill.* We suggest that *to* in this situation is a property of *Jill*, a property that *Jill has*, rather like an email in-box, containing anything heading towards *Jill* but not quite got there yet. So, at this point we have:

- *Jill has to (wards)*

and reflect this in the semantic network C showing *Jill has to*.

But also, the *giving is to* as shown here:

- *giving is to (wards)*

We combine this final fact, together with the networks of *B* and *C* to give the semantic network of *D*.

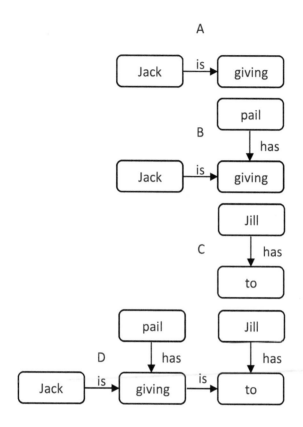

Suppose we have another variant reflected in the sentence *Jack gives Jill the pail*, with the preposition *to* absent. Is there a way of representing this on a network? One solution is to use an anonymous node. This is a node with no name associated with it. The network following shows a representation of *Jack gives Jill the pail* using such an anonymous node.

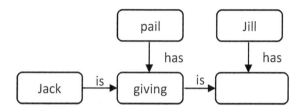

Cardinals, ordinals and quantifiers

Cardinals and ordinals

Moving on swiftly, we now have a look at cardinals and ordinals appearing in sentences.

Let's look at a typical cardinal example:

- *A lady has three cats*

Here is one way we can analyse this; there are others:

- *A lady has three cats*

- *lady has cat*
- *cat is first*
- *lady has cat*
- *cat is second*
- *lady has cat*
- *cat is third*

In this analysis example, the lady is the same in all cases, and there are pairs of *is-has cat* expressions, each referring to a different *cat*. Note that each *is* expression now introduces an ordinal e.g., *first, second, third* and so on, referencing the associated *cat*.

Below is the semantic network representation of these expressions:

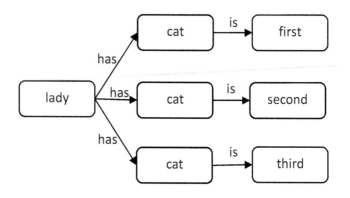

Here is an example following on from the previous:

• *The second cat is wayward*

The *cats* are identified as the *first, second* and *third*. So, we can analyse the sentence like this:

- *The second cat is wayward*
  - *cat is second*
  - *cat is wayward*

Note that this sentence is referring to data provided by the previous sentence, which is where, in *Part II Dialogues & Mental Models*, we will see that the mental model starts to come in, and we start to see the potential for melding information from one sentence with that from another.

In the figure below, you can see how the semantic network is modified by the second sentence:

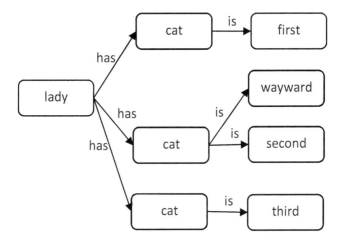

From this, we start to get some idea of how a mental model may be established and then modified by new information.

Further illustrating the modelling of cardinals, the sentences *two ladies each has two cats, each cat has two toys* result in the relationships and semantic network following. Here two *lady* nodes are present, each associated with two *cat* nodes, each with two *toy* nodes, giving a total of two *ladies*, four *cats* and eight *toys*.

We may then use ordinals to select a *toy*, with a sentence such as *the second toy of the first cat of the second lady is broken*. In practice, we work backwards through clauses, selecting the *lady* first at the tree root, then the *cat* branch, and finally the *toy* branch.

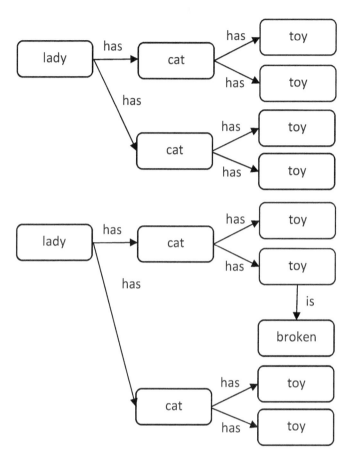

The previous example is not the only way of representing a cardinal. Here is another way:

- *A lady has three cats*
  - *lady has cat*
  - *cat is three*

Note that the plural of *cat* i.e. *cats*, has been discarded. We hope that you will agree that the plural is really only a redundant syntactic feature. The presence of *three* enables us to deduce that *cat* is plural. Here is its semantic network representation:

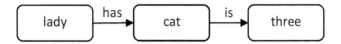

Here the opportunity to introduce ordinals referencing individual *cat*s has been lost, and generally because of this, in the model we would not use this type of representation.

Quantifiers

Associated with cardinals and ordinals we have so-called quantifiers. Quantifiers may be associated with so-called countable or uncountable items (Seely, Countable and uncountable nouns, 2004).

Consider the sentences *the hill has a tree, the hill has trees, the hill has grass,* and *the hill has grasses.* The semantic networks are shown following in *A, B, C* and *D*, respectively, and reflect how countable and uncountable items may be dealt with.

The integer or quantity flagging shown facilitates recovery of the original sentence with appropriate plurals, from the semantic network; sentence synthesis from such a network is covered in a later section on *Sentence synthesis*. If flagging is absent as in *A*, then we know a single item is referred to. If flagging is present as in *B, C* and *D*, then we know a countable or uncountable item is referred to. The difference between the two is determined by the integer flagging as in *B* and *D* (countable), or quantity flagging as in *C* (uncountable). These are just conventions used in the later described software implementation; there is nothing in the rules of

English grammar dictating these measures.

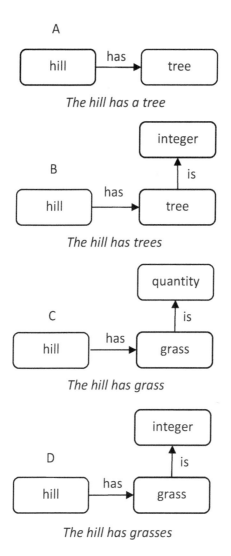

A

The hill has a tree

B

The hill has trees

C

The hill has grass

D

The hill has grasses

Ordering, sequences, and lists

Let's now move on and have a look at one or two sentences relating to arithmetic and temporal ordering. In arithmetic, we know that one, two and three occur one after another, and we can express these relationships with the following sentences, shown together with their analyses:

- *two is the successor of one*
    - *one has successor (successor of one)*
    - *two is successor*
- *three is the successor of two*
    - *two has successor (successor of two)*
    - *three is successor*
- *two is the predecessor of three*
    - *three has predecessor (predecessor of three)*
    - *two is predecessor*
- *one is the predecessor of two*
    - *two has predecessor (predecessor of two)*
    - *one is predecessor*

You will perhaps notice possible ambiguities here because of the way we sometimes express things. For example, we can say *two is successor* or *successor is two*. Glossing over these, the semantic network for the previous analysis is shown following.

We can develop similar networks for anything that has ordering associated with it e.g., the alphabet. We can also use them for expressions such as *bigger than* or *less than* e.g., if *A is bigger than B* then *B is less than A*, and so on.

These networks may be involved in logic operations e.g., if *A is bigger than B* and *B is bigger than C* then *A is bigger than C*. But these consideration lie outside the remit of this particular discourse.

We can also use a similar network to represent a sequence of events represented by a series of sentences such as:

- *Jack climbs the hill*
- *next, Jack finds the spring*
- *Jill watches Jack*
- *next, Jack fills the pail*

But we are going to defer this aspect of ordering until the *Part II* section *Sequences of events*.

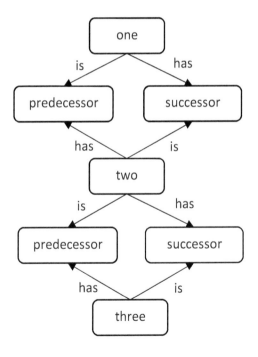

Clauses

We now have a look at more complex sentences again, and these are sentences with clauses.

Let's consider the example:

• *a balloon that is bright red has a string that is long, with a knot*

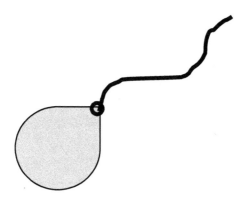

Here, the phrases

> - *that is bright red*
> and
> - *that is long*
> and
> - *with a knot*

are all clauses.

Here is the sentence analysis:

• *a balloon that is bright red has a string that is long, with a knot*
> - *balloon is red*
> - *red is bright*
> - *balloon has string*

- *string is long*
- *string has knot*

We hope that you can see here that the clauses do not influence the sentence analysis, which is exactly the same as in the very first example at the beginning of this *Part* of the book.

But, importantly, although clause addition has not influenced our *is-has* analysis, the changed phrase order has enabled aspects of our own personal view of the significance of the *balloon* and its colour and its *string* to be reflected in the sentence.

Later on, we will return to a more detailed discussion of this very significant aspect of sentence construction.

A further example

In the sentence *the balloon of the boy with the broken leg with the puncture is dark red*, the main subject is the *balloon* and the subject clauses are *of the boy* and *with the broken leg* and *with the puncture*. The clause *of the boy* refers to *the balloon*, and the clause *with the broken leg* refers to *the boy* and the clause *with the puncture* refers to *the balloon* again. The *with* in each clause is another *has*-type relation, giving a result like *boy has broken leg*. The *of* also results in a *has*-type relation as mentioned often before. The subject *the balloon of the boy with the broken leg with the puncture* gives the semantic network *A*, and the object *dark red* the network *B*.

You will notice the ambiguities reflected in these clauses. We could enforce the use commas between clauses to resolve these and clarify the meaning. In *the balloon of the boy with the broken leg, with the puncture* we could impose a rule that the comma above, separating the clauses *with the broken leg* and *with the puncture* makes the latter refer to *the balloon* and not *the boy*. This is the method that is used in the present versions of the *AI Dialog* software demonstrator, which has its limitations.

In our case, particularly with spoken sentences, we have to use our world knowledge to resolve such ambiguities. We know from our world knowledge that *with the puncture* is more likely to refer to the *balloon* than *the boy* or *the broken leg*, and that *with the broken leg* is more likely to refer to *the boy* than *the balloon*.

Clauses may of course occur with sentence subjects or sentence objects/complements. The object clauses associated with *the balloon has a string that is long, with a knot* which are *that is long* and *with a knot* are shown in the semantic network *C* following.

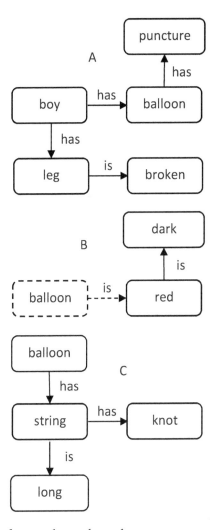

Reported speech or thoughts

Certain types of sentence cannot be handled alone by the *is-has* mechanisms so far described. A key type is where one phrase or sentence refers to another phrase, or sentence or collection of sentences.

This type requires extension to the theory previously outlined and is dealt with in much more detail later, but let's have an initial look at an example of this type of sentence.

Consider:

- *Jack says 'Jill will carry the pail'*

In this sentence, *'Jill will carry the pail'* is a sentence in its own right in the future tense. This sentence is being referred to by the phrase:

- *Jack says* (then the quotation)

Again, we need to tackle this type of problem in stages, firstly using a method resembling the *climbing* example. We begin by converting *says* to the present participle form *is saying* as shown following, and reflected in semantic network *A*.

- *Jack is saying*

Subsequently, and in the following network *B*, we make *saying* a property of *'Jill will carry the pail'*, just as *climbing* was a property of *hill* in an earlier example.

- *'Jill will carry the pail' has saying (saying of 'Jill will carry the pail')*

Now we have *'Jill will carry the pail' has saying*, which by *has/of* transformation is like *the saying of 'Jill will carry the pail'*. We then combine the two components as in the network *C* following.

Then we can move on to analyse the quoted sentence as follows:

- *Jill will carry the pail*
  - *(future)*
  - *Jill is carrying*
  - *pail has carrying (carrying of pail)*

From this we get the semantic network *D*. As remarked earlier, *Jill will carry the pail* is in the future tense or context.

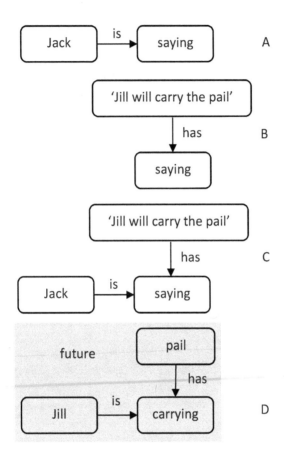

Another example

Consider the sentence *Jill thinks that Jack is dreaming*. Again, *Jack is dreaming* is another sentence in its own right, being referred to by the phrase:

- *Jill thinks that* (reported thought)

We again convert *Jill thinks* to the participle form *Jill is thinking*. *Jill* then becomes a member of a *thinking* set as in semantic network *A*. Following network *B*, we make *thinking* a property of *Jack is dreaming*, to give '*Jack is dreaming*' has *thinking* or the inverted form *the thinking of 'Jack is dreaming*'. Again, we combine two components as in network *C*. The word *that* in the sentence is discarded, as it is just a clause introducer.

The same logic also applies to sentences such as *Jill thinks/believes/hopes that Jack is dreaming* and so on; only the verb and resulting participle changes in the semantic network.

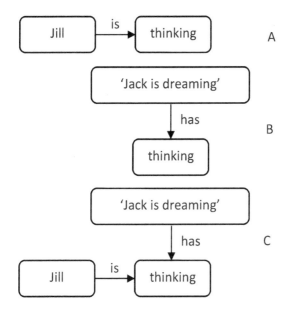

A further example

Here is a rather more subtle example of reported thoughts:

> • *It is a truth universally acknowledged, that a single man in possession of a good fortune must be in want of a wife.*

From *Pride & Prejudice - Jane Austen* (Austen, 2003)

The text:

• *a single man in possession of a good fortune must be in want of a wife*

is again a sentence in its own right, which may be analysed using the techniques previously described. The phrase *it is a truth universally acknowledged, that* (text) refers to this sentence. This is clearer if we change it to the vastly simplified phrase *people believe that* which shows it to be a reported belief. So, by taking substantial liberties with *Miss Austen,* we can simplify the sentence to give:

• *people believe, a single man who has a good fortune wants a wife.*

So, we have the analysis firstly as:

• *people believe, a single man who has a good fortune wants a wife.*
> - *people is believing*
> - *'a single man who has a good fortune wants a wife' has believing (believing of 'a single man who has a good fortune wants a wife')*

followed by:

• *a single man who has a good fortune wants a wife*
> - *man has fortune*
> - *man is single*
> - *fortune is good*
> - *man is wanting*
> - *wife has wanting (wanting of wife)*

Logical expressions

and/or

Let's move swiftly on now to look at a rather different topic: logical expressions. In practice, we find that logical expressions mostly occur in sentences representing mental model queries and, as such, are dealt with in *Part II*. But on occasions they appear in other sentence types, for example *the balloon is either red and white or blue and yellow*. Here we are expressing some informational uncertainty using an *and-or* logical expression. There are various ways of representing this in a semantic network. In practice, this may be chosen for computational convenience within the AI software, which lies beyond our considerations here, and is dealt with to a limited extent in *Part IV*. Here is one method of representation:

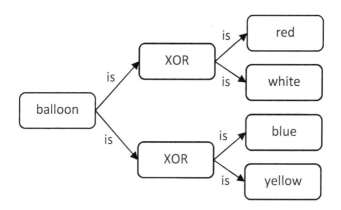

The exclusive *or XOR* is used above because the word *either* in the sentence implies one choice or the other, not both. The *balloon* is either *red and white* or *blue and yellow*, never neither or both. A similar construction may be used for the inclusive *or OR* if the word *either* is absent.

if-then expressions

These are expressions such as *if the balloon has a long string then it is yellow* or *if the balloon has a short string then it is red*. Again these are mostly likely to occur in sentences representing mental model operations and detailed considerations are deferred to *Part II*.

But anyway, there is a tendency for these to be subsumed by equivalent expressions such as *each balloon with a long string is yellow* or *each balloon with a long string is red*. They may occur as stored undecoded strings constituting stored instructions and similar data. Here is a typical semantic network for one:

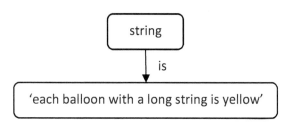

The passive voice

Here we have a brief look at the effect on the semantic network of a sentence cast in the passive voice (Seely, Passive voice, 2004). The passive voice is generally used for one of two reasons.

The first is to emphasise some aspect of the sentence. For example, instead of saying *Jack is climbing the hill*, we might say *the hill is being climbed by Jack*, bringing the *hill* into prominence rather than *Jack*. In this case there is no effect on the semantic network; both forms give the same network, as shown in *A* following.

The second reason is to depersonalise things, and is

commonly used in scientific or technical writing e.g., we might say *the temperature was taken*. We are not interested in who took the *temperature*; it's irrelevant. Our passive variant of the earlier sentence would be *the hill is being climbed*; Jack has been removed from consideration. The problem is: how do we represent this on the network?

There are various solutions and *B* following shows one. We again make use of the anonymous node as in the earlier section *Direct & indirect objects*. The figure shows the *hill has climbing (climbing of hill)* but rather than *Jack is climbing*, we have (*anonymous) is climbing*. The anonymous node reflects our lack of information; we know someone, or something is *climbing*, but we do not know any more.

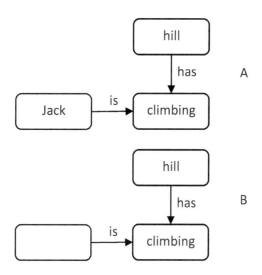

isnt and *hasnt*

The *isnt* and *hasnt* relations allow us to negate the action of *is* and *has*, respectively. Note that for simplicity we omit the apostrophe in these expressions. Again these are mostly likely to occur in sentences representing mental model operations, and detailed considerations are deferred to *Part II*. Examples are *each child who isnt tired climbs the hill* or *each child who hasnt a balloon is unhappy*. Applicable to general verbs are *didnt*, *doesnt* and *wont*, as in *Jack wont climb the hill*. It is theoretically possible to eliminate these types of expression by interpreting *not* as an adverb, as for example in *the balloon is not blue*, which gives the *is-has* relations *balloon is blue* and *blue is not*.

Semantic information and syntax

When we start to extract the semantic information from a sentence, we need to recognise that much English syntax carries no semantic information. To build the semantic network-based model of the sentence we must strip out redundant syntax, and retain just the essential semantics.

For example, we say *I am, you are, he is* instead of *I is, you is, he is*. The latter sounds strange but does retain the semantics, allowing just *is* instance relations and corresponding edges to be used on the model, simplifying it. Similar considerations apply to *I have, you have, he has* which reduce to *I has, you has, he has*. Other declinations associated with tense e.g., *was* or *had*, disappear because, as we have seen in this *Part*, we make use of contexts to handle tense, and within each context only the third person present tense need be used.

A further example is use of plurals, which again largely represent purely syntactic information, and which is generally semantically redundant. If we say *three cats*, we really know *cat(s)* is plural because of the *three*. We could just say *three cat*. In practice we are able to eliminate plurals and retain only singulars on the model. You will have observed earlier that all network instances/nodes are singular. This simplifies the isomorphic searches, described later; when we search for an instance, we need to consider only its singular. You have seen that with an example such as *two toffees*, we are able to represent each *toffee* separately; we have two individual *toffee* instances, and the plural disappears. But occasionally the plural is significant as in *Jack has some apple* c.f. *Jack has some apples*. However, we have shown that we can avoid quantified plurals as in these examples by adding *quantity* and *number* node flagging to the model, as described earlier under *Cardinals, ordinals, and quantifiers*.

Another example is comparators. We say, *Jack is taller than Jill* but we could say, *Jack is tall than Jill* dropping the *er* ending, regularising the adjective *tall*, whilst the syntax remains recoverable due to the word *than*.

Indefinite and definite articles such as *a/an*, *the*, or *each* do carry semantic information but need not appear in their original form on the model. Their significance is discussed later.

Anaphoric references never need appear on the model because *he has the pail*, for example, is replaced by *Jack has the pail*, and so on. This means none of the pronouns *he, she, they* or *it* need ever appear on the model. Similar considerations apply to possessive versions of pronouns, that is *his (Jack has …), hers (Jill has …), their (each pail has), its (the pail has …)* and so on. This also applies to accusative versions of pronouns, that is *him (Jack), her (Jill), them (each …)* and *it*.

Another example of an anaphoric reference which appears in sentences, but does not need any representation on the model is the word *latter*. For example, if we have *A lady has a Siamese cat and a Burmese cat*, we may later say, not necessarily contiguously, *the latter cat is happy* identifying the *Burmese cat*.

It almost goes without saying that sentence punctuation need not be present on the model e.g. the initial capital at a sentence start or the full stop at its end. Commas and semicolons do often carry significant semantic information but do not appear directly on the model. This topic is mentioned again later in *Part IV* under *Adjective/adverb strings*.

Although, as we've just seen, plurals, indefinite and definite articles, and anaphoric references are absent on our model, this doesn't prevent us from synthesising grammatically correct sentences from the model, when we need to. When sentences are synthesised from the model, enough information remains to regenerate the required syntax. We know *I* takes *am* and *you* takes *are* and *he* retains *is*. We also still have enough information on the model to form *cats* from *cat*, or to form *a/an* or *the/each* as needed, or to abbreviate *Jack* to *he* or *him* when appropriate, and so on. Sentence synthesis from the model is discussed in detail later in *Part II* under *Sentence synthesis*, where we also discuss regenerating sentence stress associated with sentence word order.

In conclusion, the previous are just a few examples of redundant sentence syntax which does not need to be reflected on the sentence semantic network model.

Miscellaneous examples of sentence analysis

Towards the conclusion of this section, here are a few more sentence analysis examples:

> • *Patriotism, is the last refuge of a scoundrel* - Samuel Johnson (Wikipedia, 2021)

> • *Patriotism, is the last refuge of a scoundrel*
>> - *refuge is last*
>> - *scoundrel has refuge*
>> - *refuge is patriotism* (the object precedes the

subject here)

• *This is the beginning of a beautiful friendship* - Humphrey Bogart – Casablanca (Curtiz, 1942)

• *This is the beginning of a beautiful friendship*
> - *friendship is beautiful*
> - *friendship has beginning (beginning of friendship)*
> - *this is beginning*

• *In Xanadu did Kubla Khan A stately pleasure dome decree* - Samuel Taylor Coleridge – Kubla Khan (Coleridge, 1983)

Ignoring the past tense, and assuming the present tense for now:

• *In Xanadu did Kubla Khan A stately pleasure dome decree*
> - *Khan is Kubla*
> - *dome has pleasure (pleasure-dome* effectively*)*
> - *dome is stately*
> - *Khan is decreeing*
> - *dome has decreeing (decreeing of dome)*
> - *Xanadu has in(side)*
> - *dome is in(side)*

Colloquial expressions

As a final point just before approaching the conclusion of this *Part*. Colloquial expressions are where the words used, and the actual meaning differ. So, if we have *Jack* says *stone the crows, this pail is heavy*, we know that *Jack* is not suggesting ornithological cruelty, but that his pronouncement is actually a complaint about the *heaviness* of the *pail*. This could be represented in various ways. One possibility is shown in the semantic network following:

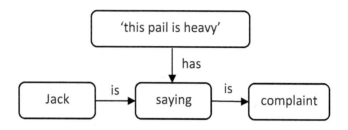

Colloquial expressions generally cannot be analysed, they just have to have their real meanings known and listed for use by the semantic analysis software. In practice, we humans learn their meanings, either by being told them, or by deducing them from the situations of their usage in sentences we read or hear.

Philosophical aspects of is-has analysis

Implications

Hopefully, by now you will be convinced that sentence *is-has* analysis does actually work. If you find that you can believe that this type of analysis is valid, and of course you may choose not to do so, but if you do, then we suggest that there are a number significant philosophical implications to this. We begin to discuss these in the following sections of the book.

Prescriptive grammar

You may have realised that many of the parts of speech arising in prescriptive grammatical analysis typified by Fowler (Butterfield, 2015), such as the subject, the predicate, nouns, adjectives, adverbs, prepositions, and so on, are often subsumed in the *is-has* form of analysis. Even verbs tend to lose their central position, and in fact mostly disappear altogether during the analysis; the only remaining verbs are the third person declinations of *to be* and *to have* i.e. *is* and *has*.

Not quite new

You may wonder if the method of sentence analysis shown here in this text is entirely new. The answer is: not quite. In the 17th century the Messieurs de Port Royale, a group of academic Catholic monks in a publication entitled *A general and rational Grammar* (Arnauld & Lancelot, 1753 translation) amongst many other things, analysed the sentence *the invisible God created the visible world* as follows:

> • *the invisible God created the visible world.*
>> - *God is invisible*
>> - *God created the world*
>> - *the world is visible*

Here we go much further by decomposing phrases such as *God created the world* too as:

>> - *(past)*
>> - *world has creating (creating of world)*
>> - *God is creating*

Loss of Information

Is there a loss of information in our analyses, you may well ask. There certainly is. The following sentences:

> • *Jack is climbing the hill*
> • *the climbing of the hill is by Jack*
> • *the hill is being climbed by Jack*

all have the same analysis:

- *Jack is climbing*
- *hill has climbing (climbing of hill)*

We have lost the stresses in the original sentences, showing the topics we considered to be most important by putting them in significant positions in their respective sentences i.e., *Jack* or *the climbing* or *the hill*. The facts have been retained but the speaker's opinions of these facts have been lost.

It is possible to retain this information during sentence syntax analysis and to subsequently represent it on the semantic network e.g., by adding *climbing is significant* to the semantic network. This is not done with the present software and involves complications, discussions of which are beyond the remit of the present discourse.

In a later section in *Part II, Sentence synthesis*, we discuss how it is possible to perform the inverse operation of adding a stress-dependent word order to a sentence synthesised from a mental model.

Another aspect of information loss is associated with temporal aspects. If we mention *Jack* in a sentence and then shortly afterwards use the anaphoric reference *he*, then we can generally deduce that *he* means *Jack*. However, if there is a significant period of time and/or other things being discussed then the tie between *Jack* and *he* may weaken or be lost altogether. We could help to address this issue by time-stamping nodal data on a mental model. This is not done at present.

The nature of *to be* and *to have*

Moving on now, the question must arise, what is so significant about *to be* and *to have* that their third person declinations *is* and *has* are such dominant components in our analyses of sentences?

Before attempting to answer this question, we must dispose of a couple of issues.

To do

The first issue is that the main auxiliary verbs in English are based on *to be*, *to have* and *to do*.

So, is there any reason why *to do* has not been involved in our analyses? One reason was partly covered in the earlier section on *Semantic issues surrounding participles*. There, we made a conscious choice not to involve *to do* largely because we felt we could manage without it, as its function could be encompassed by *to be*. So, instead of saying *Jack does climb the hill*, we could say *Jack is climbing the hill*. But *is* could be used for other purposes too, whereas *does* could not e.g., *the balloon is red*, *Jack is a doctor* and so on. This choice therefore minimised our semantic operators or the labels required on semantic network edges.

Reviewing the uses of *to do* in sentences, we use declinations of *to do* as an auxiliary verb in the formation of:

- negatives (*Jack doesnt climb up the hill*)
- questions (*does Jack climb up the hill?*)
- and emphatics (*Jack does climb up the hill*)

In these:

- negatives (*Jack doesnt climb up the hill*)
- and questions (*does Jack climb up the hill?*)

are associated with dynamic operations on the mental model, the former with assertions, and the latter with queries, and consideration of these uses is deferred to *Part II*.

This then leaves:

> • emphatics (*Jack does climb up the hill*)

which are simply discarded, as they just represent a personal view or opinion of a situation which is never reflected in the semantic network.

However, *to do* on occasions appears as a verb in its own right, as in:

> • *Jack is doing the washing*

which gives:

> - *Jack is doing*
> - *washing has doing* (*doing of washing*)

In these instances, the semantic network is derived in the usual way with *doing* being the participle.

Definitions

The second issue is the big, big difference in the meaning of *is* in:

> • *Jack is tall*
> and
> • *Jack is a doctor*

The addition of a determiner, after *is*, in this case the indefinite article *a* in:

> • *Jack is a doctor*

as opposed to its absence in:
* *Jack is tall*

completely changes the meaning of the verb.

Note also that *doctor* is a noun whilst *tall* is an adjective.

In the case of:

* *Jack is tall*

we have the association of the simple *tallness* property with *Jack*.

But in the case of:

* *Jack is a doctor*

we have a much more complex situation.

Somewhere, either in our minds, on paper, or elsewhere is a concept or a definition of a *doctor*.

So, we may feel:

* *a doctor is kind*
* *a doctor is compassionate*
* *a doctor has a degree*
* *the degree is medical*

and so on.

So, we have a mental list of things that a *doctor is* and a list of things that a *doctor has*.

When we say:

- *Jack is a doctor*

We cause *Jack* to potentially inherit all these attributes.

By using the shorthand of:

- *Jack is a doctor*

it avoids us having to say:

- *Jack is kind*
- *Jack is compassionate*
- *Jack has a degree*
- *the degree is medical*

and so on.

But we have to be careful, because sometimes the determiner, in the previous case *a*, is absent, and just implied.

For example, we may say:

- *Aristotle is Greek*

rather than

- *Aristotle is a Greek*

We can sometimes spot this by checking if the complement is a proper noun rather than an adjective.

Having dispensed with these two issues, let us now return to the consideration of the nature of *to be* and *to have*.

To be

Consider first the very much simpler concept of:

- *to be*

We are going to begin by suggesting that *to be* tends to very much find use with things that we directly sense. For example:

> sight and sound:
> • *is bright, is red, is round, is loud, is tuneful*
> and other senses:
> • *is hot, is painful, is hungry, is thirsty*
> or sensed emotions:
> • *is happy, is excited, is depressed*

Significantly, some of the things we sense can be quite complex or dynamic, and will require more computation in the mind and brain than others for example:

> • *is circular*
> • *is fast or slow*
> • *is running*

In the case of concepts such as *fast* and *slow* and *running*, we have to take mental snapshots of something at a number of intervals and then compare these snapshots.

We suggest we can also divide things we directly sense into internally sensed things, for example, emotions or pain and so on, and those based on externally sensed things, for example, colours, sounds, visual patterns, and so on.

Shortly, in connection with the later section entitled: *The origins of human language,* we are going to suggest exactly why *to be* is for things we directly sense. But for now, we are going to move on to consider *to have*.

To have

We are going to begin by suggesting that *to have* is a

phenomenally complex and powerful concept.

We are going to suggest that the concept of *having* forms the basis of all of our mathematics, science, and engineering.

Why do we claim this?

Once we start to embrace the concept of *to have* or *having*, then we are grappling with the concept that a thing can be composed of subsidiary parts, that a component can be composed of sub-components, that a heap or group can have individual members.

Once we use the expression *X has Y* we are flagging that *Y* is a part or sub-component or member of the thing *X*. Here, *X* could be a tree, a leaf, an individual person, a group of people, a geographical feature, a belief, a theory, a mathematical set, in fact anything at all. What we are saying is that we appreciate that whatever thing we choose, it is composed of separable parts or components. We are identifying one of those parts or components and asserting that it belongs to the whole thing. In doing this, we have to vitally, perceive both the whole thing and the component part at the same time.

If we do not have this concept of the whole thing and the part at the same time, then we suggest that the only way we can select one part or component of a thing, is by getting sufficiently close to it physically, visually, or mentally, so that the one part or the one component alone completely fills our sensory (typically visual) field. We have effectively mentally zoomed in on it. But by this point, we have lost all concept of the whole thing. We have the severe mental limitation that we are unable to perceive both the whole thing and the part or component of the thing both at the same time.

However, once we have the concept that a thing can be split up into parts, then we soon realise that a part we have selected can also be split up into further parts, and when we have selected one of these, into further parts, and so on. We begin to realise that we can iterate this process to any depth we choose.

So, we suggest that a large part of physics is concerned with recognising that things may be split into parts, that may be split up into further parts, and into further parts, and so on.

But once we have the previous concept, then we suggest that there is another very closely related concept that we can start to encompass. This concept is the inverse of the previous concept, and it the concept of being able to assemble a number of parts or components into what we then conceive as a new whole thing.

But we suggest that this concept leads us into arithmetic. If we merge one lot of parts with another lot of parts and regard the resulting lot of parts as a whole thing, then we have moved towards addition.

If we remove some parts from a set of parts we have constituting a whole thing and regard the result as a new whole thing, then we have moved towards subtraction.

If we order the parts of an existing whole thing, and associate a different name or symbol with each part, we then we have moved towards counting.

If we start to associate names with separate whole things composed of parts, we have moved towards algebra. And very soon, algebra leads us into higher mathematics.

So, we strongly suggest that the deceptively simple concept

of appreciating that a whole thing may split into component parts, and also the inverse concept that a whole thing may be assembled from component parts has the phenomenal potential to lead us into all our physics, mathematics, engineering, and scientific technology generally.

We must never underestimate the phenomenal power of the concept of:

- *to have*

which is able to link in our minds and in a mental model a component part with a whole thing composed of other such component parts.

The real nature of verbs

The dictionary defines a verb as:

- *a part of speech which asserts or predicates something*

We suggest that this does not get us very far.

Instead, we also encounter the definition:

- *a word that describes an action (or a state of being)*

Let's defer consideration of the concept of *state of being* for a moment or two; we will discuss it shortly.

So, let's go back to the original verb example of *Jack climbs*, with the participle form *Jack is climbing*.

We noted that if *Jack* was in outer space away from any celestial or manufactured object, as shown following, then *Jack* would not be able to *climb* anything.

Jack, as shown further following, needs a *climbing* environment for *climbing* to be possible.

We suggest it is impossible for us to visualise *Jack is climbing*, without our minds automatically providing a vestigial imagined environment within which the *climbing* becomes possible. We briefly mentioned this point in the earlier section *Semantic issues surrounding participles* when we gave the example of the bald sentence *Jack is climbing* which does not say what he is *climbing*.

We suggest this situation exists for the majority of verbs. Most verbs demand an environment within which the action described by the verb is feasible.

The act of *walking* demands a *walking* surface. The act of *talking* demands air in which sound waves can be propagated, and so on.

We get so wrapped up in the actor performing the verb's action, and the nature of the action itself, we forget the essential environment that is needed for the action described to take place.

We suggest we can now redefine most verbs along the following lines:

> • *A verb is a word that describes an action taking place within an environment capable of supporting that action.*

State of being

Let's now return to a consideration of the *state of being*. There are a large number of verbs where the thing or person performing the action is the same as the thing or person providing the environment to support that action. Consider the following sentence *the engine is running*. Here the *engine* is performing the action i.e., it is using the verb *to run*. But the *engine* is also providing the environment to make the *running* action possible. We could use an analysis as shown below and in *A* of the following network.

- *the engine is running*
  - *engine is running*
  - *engine has running (running of engine)*

But in practice, all the information required is represented in the analysis shown below and in *B* in the network.

- *the engine is running*
  - *engine is running*

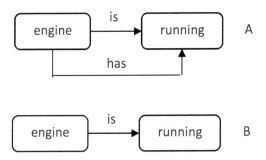

There are many other examples of this situation exemplified by the sentences *the heart is beating, the circuit is oscillating, the kettle is boiling* and so on. But as we have shown above, they are representable by an appropriate semantic network, and, as we will see later, can be accommodated within a mental model.

The origins of human language

If we accept that sentences are reducible to sequences of *is* and *has* expressions then we may be able to speculate on the origins of human language.

Is it just possible that sentences are reducible to *is* and *has* expressions because each sentence we speak or write now is actually a coalescent of completely separate *is* and *has* utterances existing at the dawn of human language.

In other words, is it possible to break sentences down into a series of separate *is* and *has* expressions, because:

- at the dawn of human language,
- that's how they started out

as a series of separate discrete *is* and *has* utterances.

We can imagine that gradually sequences of separate discrete *is* and *has* utterances merged together to become sentences – because it facilitated more rapid speech and thereby communication. We suggest that the forces of evolution would tend to take us along this course. Humans that could communicate with each other more rapidly would have an evolutionary advantage over others communicating less rapidly. So, perhaps that is why we can take a sentence now and, with some thought, break it back down into the original *is* and *has* expressions.

Of course, cramming more and more information into the same communications bandwidth is exactly what happens today with modern electronics. This is facilitated by progressively more complex encoding of the transmitted data. But there are trade-offs here which probably affect human speech and writing too. More complex encoding requires more computation by the transmitter to encode the data and by the receiver to decode it. There are also the physical limitations of the voice box and ear and the capacity of the air to propagate sound, in terms of both frequency and distance. Highly encoded data also suffers from higher rates of transmission errors.

To be frank, although we might assess what physical transmitter, receiver, and media constraints might apply with human beings, we do not really know whether the brain might impose computational constraints, on how quickly it can encode mental concepts for transmission and decode received data into the corresponding concepts.

Resuming our main arguments again now, let's postulate three foundations for human language. The first two we suggest are features of many of the lower animals. The last is just a feature of ourselves and possibly some other hominids. So here we go.

Firstly, a sense of sequence.

• event A is often followed by event B

Event A is often followed by event B. Sometimes described as a sense of causality. Your dog gets excited when you pick up the lead.

You can see the evolutionary advantage for any organism of being able to predict future events based on present events.

We suggest this leads to a sense of past, present, and future, that is a sense of tense.

If you think about it, any organism capable of detecting new event sequences needs quite sophisticated biological hardware and software.

It has to keep a substantial record of events, and then do complex statistical analysis on this record to detect that B often follows A.

Even more complex analysis is needed to detect B follows A

as long as *C* isn't present, and so on.

Secondly, the *is* expression.

> • *I am hungry; I am hurt; I am angry; there is danger*

Primitive animal cries reflect things the animal directly senses *hungry! hurt! go away! danger!*

One can imagine that with the coming of greater human vocal ability, these cries could become more sophisticated and become the *is* expressions we know.

Thirdly, the *has* expression.

> • something is composed of separate identifiable parts

We have already extensively discussed the nature of this possibly unique human or hominid concept and the possible reasons why we have been able to develop science and technology from it.

To these three foundations, we must add the concepts of *each* and *is a* … which involve consideration of a mental model, and are subjects explored in *Part II Dialogues & Mental Models*.

Language universals

We may hypothesise, but admittedly entirely without any experimental evidence, that *is* and *has* are universal mental concepts totally independent of any particular language, and are fundamental components of how human minds work everywhere. If this is true, then ultimately all human languages, irrespective of syntax or semantics may be based on them. They may be language universals.

There are of course one or two very obvious equivalents in

languages closely related to English, for example, *is* and *has* equivalents in French (*est* and *a*), German (*ist* and *hat*) and Italian (*e* and *ha*) all used in pretty much the same way we use them in English, and therefore susceptible to the same sort of mental model building we are about to describe in *Part II*. Determining if these concepts are extendible to other Indo-European languages, and indeed to all World languages would be an extremely interesting research topic for someone.

Technical aspects of is-has analysis

This section discusses various technical aspect of analysing sentences using *is-has* technology, and you can skip it if you wish.

Let's begin this discussion by suggesting that the traditional approach to the science of linguistics has been focussed on first tackling the syntactic aspects of human language i.e., the word structures and patterns contained within sentences and phrases, but deferring the semantic aspects until the problems of the former have hopefully been solved.

We suggest that this is because syntactics has tended to be more approachable. There is a vast feedstock of written and spoken language available for analysis. The problems of semantics and the apparently mind-numbing problem of trying to determine the meaning of meaning has tended to discourage investigation. A while ago it was reported that one academic institution had ceased the teaching of linguistic semantics because of the intellectual challenges involved.

It is true too that a proportion of practical problems, particularly those involving the search for information on the web can be solved by looking principally just at the syntactic content of sentences and ignoring the semantic. For example, suppose we encounter a sentence representing a question answerable by certain data on the web. We can analyse the question purely syntactically noting that it contains particular word patterns. We can then search for syntactic relatives or variants of these patterns on the web. For any that we find, we can reply to the question with a proportion of the text surrounding the located patterns. In many cases this will result in a satisfactory answer to the question. So, the whole process can been carried out without any real understanding of the question's semantic content.

Sentence analysis generally involves so-called parsing, which means splitting the sentence, or a phase within the sentence, into significant components. Such components may be phrases or individual words. If they are phrases then we can continue the process, until every element of the sentence has been dealt with. The principal types of sentence analysis are termed Constituency (Wikipedia, 2023), Error-Repair (Lyon, 1974) and Dependency (Wikipedia, 2023). These are all largely syntactically based.

Constituency analysis is not far removed from the classical sentence syntax analysis based on the grammatical rules given in Fowler's Dictionary of English (Fowler & Fowler, 1989). Error-Repair analysis is similar to Constituency analysis with some in-built dynamic flexibility to allow some relaxation or variation of grammatical rules if a given sentence comes close to, but does not quite fit them. It is effectively treating the sentence as if it contained syntactic errors. Dependency analysis depends on finding links or dependencies between pairs of sentence words.

The closest relative to *is-has* analysis amongst the methods mentioned is Dependency analysis since both are concerned with looking for links between pairs of sentence words. However, here the comparison ends. All of the previous methods attempt to parse the raw input sentence. In contrast, *is-has* analysis carries out substantial, mainly lexical processing of the sentence before attempting to parse. Some of this processing is referenced in the earlier section *Semantic information and syntax,* and elsewhere, and includes conversion of verb or noun plurals to singular, conversion of verbs to participle form, conversion of anaphoric references, extraction of tense, insertion of implied but absent *has/of* words and many other measures. Notably, in sharp contrast with the other techniques mentioned, *is* and *has* always appear as edges rather than nodes on the *is-has* parse graph.

The basic philosophy behind the *is-has* analysis and parse is the theory that sentences consist entirely of *is-has* expressions that over time have become squeezed together and truncated as humans tried to cram more and more information into sentences, to optimise intercommunication. The job of the *is-has* parse is to expand back to the original *is-has* expressions by unsqueezing expressions and nullifying truncations – generally involving the addition of *is* and *has* and *of* semantic operators.

Conclusion

This is the conclusion of *Part I* of the book. In *Part II*, coming next we show how we can build a mental model from parts of a dialogue composed of a succession or group of sentences, and how this then gives us a path to artificial general intelligence, sometimes referred to as strong AI.

The theory in *Part I* is supported by a *YouTube®* lecture of about one hour duration, entitled *Artificial General Intelligence, A New Approach, Part I Sentence Semantics.*

(This page is intentionally blank)

PART II

DIALOGUES & MENTAL MODELS

Definition of the mental model

Let's look at mental models first. There are various definitions of a mental model sometimes referred to as an ontology (Hofweber, 2018). Here we define a mental model as a simplified abstraction or representation of the real world which we hold in our minds to assist us in our lives. Exactly what this involves will become more apparent as we proceed.

We are used to the idea of using models for forecasting purposes. So, we have economic models used for forecasting economic performance, meteorological models used to forecast the weather, and so on. A characteristic of these models is that their internal components are designed for the job which the model does. It is not generally possible to use an economic model to forecast the weather or a meteorological model to forecast economic performance. The functionality of their components is designed for their specific fields of application.

When we come to a human mental model, we are faced with the problem that the human mind can think and calculate and reason about almost anything, about the economy, the weather, the air flow over an airfoil, the organisation of a company, even our projected visit to the supermarket, literally anything. If we are to contemplate a mental model that can encompass any of these contemplatable things, then its internal components must be based on some non-specific, non-application-orientated, exceptionally general-purpose abstraction.

In early school we encountered reading comprehension exercises, involving reading and comprehending a simple description of something, followed by responding to queries testing our comprehension. For example:

- *A lady has two Burmese cats and three Siamese cats*
- *Each Burmese cat has three biscuits and two toys*
- *Each Siamese cat has two biscuits and three toys*
- *Count each lady, each cat, each biscuit, and each toy*

One method of approach for us is to build a mental model of the situation from the English sentences and then consult the model to carry out some calculation, and then to synthesise some sentences constituting replies responding to the queries. In practice, we probably re-read individual sentences and construct a number of simple sub-models to solve each part of the problem.

In this part we study mechanisms allowing computer software to do similar sorts of things. In fact, the software demonstrator *AI Dialog*, described in *Part IV*, is able to read and understand exactly the same English sentences and respond correctly to the examples just given.

Building the mental model

In practice, our own mental model is established and constantly updated using data from all of our senses. But in this book we are going to consider just a small part of this

mental model,   established, updated, and queried using an
English language dialogue or discourse, only.

In this part we are going to progress onwards from analysing
individual sentences in terms of *is* and *has* expressions to
considering sequences or groups of sentences comprising
part of a dialogue or discourse. We are going to see that by
taking each sentence in turn and breaking it down into *is* and
has expressions, we can merge or blend the information
contained in each sentence with that contained in other
sentences, to give an integrated model.

Let's now have a close look at the form of the sentences
within a discourse or dialogue, from which a mental model
may be built.

Let's begin by recognising a very significant property, that
sentences generally have two components. One component
specifies new data to add to our mental model, and another
component, whereabouts on our model. In most English
sentences, the latter component usually appears before the
former. Let's look at the sentence:

- *the Siamese cat is very fierce*

Let's assume we have heard something of a saga of a *Siamese
cat* previously, amongst perhaps tales of other *cats*. The
phrase *the Siamese cat* picks out our *Siamese cat* data location on
our model, from possibly several other cat data locations.
This particular *cat* must be *Siamese*. If there are no *Siamese cats*,
or more than one, the sentence may not be understood by us
and may be treated by us as ambiguous. Otherwise, the *is very
fierce* data is associated with the selected *cat* data location on
our model. We have added to the information we have about
the *Siamese cat*.

To put it another way, this is very much like updating an IT database. The following is an example of an update to such a database, using the IT database query language *SQL*, standing for *Structured Query Language* (McGrath, 2020).

> • *UPDATE pets SET character = 'is very fierce'*
> *WHERE breed = 'Siamese' AND type = 'cat';*

You don't really need to understand SQL to see how it resembles the structure of the previous sentence.

In practice of course, our human mental model database is far more versatile than any IT database. Our mental decoding of the content of English sentences allows for much more flexible data input. One of the big limitations of the conventional IT database is that the structure of the data any part of it is designed to hold must be known in advance. In the previous SQL example, we need to have designed in advance a table called *pets*. Each row or record in that table needs to have been designed with fields called *character*, *breed*, and *type*. A big problem with our own data is that we do not know its structure in advance; we have to be prepared to be hit with any kind of structured data.

Looking at a few more aspects of sentences; in some cases, a sentence introduces new data, and implicitly provides a location for further data, as in the sentence:

> • *a dog has a bone*

Here, *a dog* adds a location *dog* to our model, and provides that location with the data *has a bone*.

Sometimes there is no specific model location given in a sentence, as in:

- *there are three Burmese cats*

Which means we just add to our model this fact, and in practice create three new data locations for future new individual *Burmese cat* data.

Sometimes a sentence provides linkages between existing data locations. For example, if *Jack* and *hill* already exist on our mental model; we've heard about them previously; then *Jack climbs the hill* links them.

A decoding problem which arises with sentences containing many complex clause structures, is that the location on our model, and the data to be added at that location, tend to get all mixed up. Some complex sentences may in fact mention multiple model locations with multiple data updates associated with them.

For example, the sentence:

- *Jack and Jill each climbs up the steep hill*

where *Jack* and *Jill* and *steep hill* already exist on our model, involves separate updates to all three locations. The *Jack* and *Jill* locations are updated with *climbing* that is *up*, and the *steep hill* location, with the two occurrences of *climbing*. Sentences with complex clauses can involve even more convoluted updates to our model. Shortly we will examine in detail how such updates may be carried out when we implement a mental model as a component of an AI system.

A final component of a typical sentence is its truth or falsehood. In our terms, we ask: does it represent a proposed valid or invalid update of our mental model? If it is a proposed invalid update, then can we detect that this is so, and avoid adding erroneous data to our model?

This is a significant topic, dealt with only briefly here. Just a couple of points. A computer without our real-world knowledge can only determine validity in the situation of its own model, not in the situation of the real world. If a sentence a computer reads refers to a *second cat*, with only one *cat* present on its model, it can detect that this is invalid. But if a sentence declares:

- *there is a present King of France*

it generally has to assume this is valid, because its knowledge is limited to just what any discourse or dialogue contains. This is a problem discussed by Bertrand Russell (Cryan, Shatil, & Mayblin, Russell's System, 2013).

The semantic network mental model

From *Part I* you may have now started to guess that we can use a semantic network as a foundation for our AI technology implementation of a mental model.

Of course, this is not necessarily the way our own brains and minds hold our own mental model, but it does give similar results in the software execution of comprehension and other mental model manipulation exercises, as we will eventually see.

Semantic networks have a long history of use in linguistic semantics. The following figure shows a typical network, representing part of the *station* example of *Part I*.

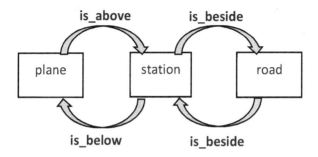

You will notice that in this example the links between the nodes represent fairly complicated concepts e.g., *is_above*, *is_beside* and *is_below*.

But in *Part I*, if you remember, we adopted a very rational semantic network representation, by using only *is* or *has* on the edges linking nodes. This became possible because we were able to suggest that all English sentences could be reduced entirely to sets of simple *is* and *has* expressions, that is, *X is Y* and *X has Y* where *X* and *Y* were mostly single words from the sentence. In the following figure we see the resulting rationalised network. You will note the use of the operable properties *above* and *below* associated with the *plane* and *station*, and the operable property *beside* associated with the *station* and the *road*.

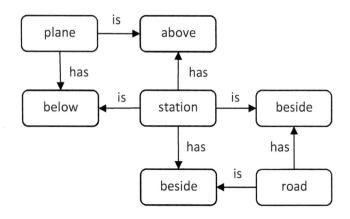

By this means we are able to avoid using complex concepts on semantic network edges linking nodes. This important key step facilitates computer processing of the resulting network, as will gradually become obvious.

Instances

A further point is that so far, we have referred to the boxes containing text which appear on our semantic network, as nodes. At this point we are also going to introduce the word *instance* to interchangeably refer to a node. So in the previous figure we have single *plane, station, road, above* and *below* instances, but two *beside* instances.

The latter point brings out a particular aspect of instances. We can have more than one node with the same name, but each node is a separate instance associated with that name. So, we can say, for example, two instances of *beside* or four instances of *cat*. As we can see, each instance is always represented by a separate node.

Each new noun and preposition, for example *plane* and *station* or *above* and *below*, in sentences is represented by a new node/instance on the semantic network. These are then connected by *is-has* relations also derived from the sentences. A vital feature of the instance is that it frees us from the concepts of nouns, adjectives, adverbs, prepositions, verbs, and other parts of speech, and enables us to handle dialogue or discourse sentence parts of speech in a purely abstract way. Something which again facilitates computation.

The discussions which follow will show how the concept of the instance can be used to help build a mental model from an English dialogue, and as we have already mentioned, enable this model to be consulted to reply to comprehension queries or perform logic or calculations. Importantly, later on, we will see how this mental model may be used to synthesise plain English replies to queries or present logic and calculation answers.

Much later, when we describe software operation in *Appendix A, The AI Dialog Demonstrator* we will encounter listings of the content of the mental model appearing in what is referred to as a *Mental Model* tab. Here, nodes/instances and their connectivity are listed. Here, in order to distinguish between nodes/instances having the same name, integers are appended to separate instances of the node name. So for four separate *cat* instances, we would have *cat(1), cat(2), cat(3)* and *cat(4)*. You will have seen that in semantic network diagrams, instance integers are not required as we can recognise from the diagrams, that separate instances are involved.

Building, updating, and querying our mental model

Let's now examine in detail the steps in building, then updating, and then querying our mental model. Again, this is not necessarily the way our mind and brain does the same job, but as we shall see, it does give us a practical technology we can study.

We are going to start using the term *subnet* for a small part of a semantic network derived from either the whole of, or just part of a sentence, and we are going to use the term *main net* or just *net* for the semantic network constituting the whole of our mental model. You will appreciate that the *main net* will change, typically getting progressively larger, as we process the successive sentences of a discourse or dialogue.

Building our mental model

Suppose the first sentence we ever encounter in building our mental model, is:

- *a lady has three cats*

The first step is to reduce this to *is* and *has* expressions alone, as we saw in *Part I*. Following therefore, from *Part I*, is the *is-has* analysis:

- *a lady has three cats*
  - *lady has cat*

- *cat is first*
- *lady has cat*
- *cat is second*
- *lady has cat*
- *cat is third*

From this we can derive the semantic network following which constitutes the initial content of our model.

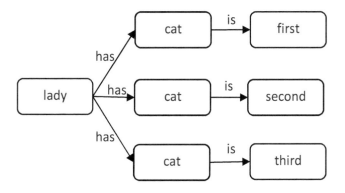

Updating our mental model

Suppose we subsequently encounter the sentence:

• *the second cat is very wayward*

This is an update or augmentation of our mental model data. How do we go about modifying the model to add this new information? Again, the first step is to reduce the sentence to *is* and *has* expressions alone. So, we have the analysis:

• *the second cat is very wayward*
  - *cat is second*

- *cat is wayward*
- *wayward is very*

This then gives us the subnet shown following:

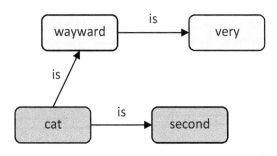

But look at the phrase:

- *the second cat*

and the corresponding part of the subnet shown in the lower part of the figure following:

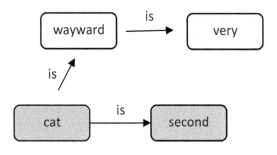

The phrase:

- the second cat

is headed by the definite article *the*, implying that what follows is something already present on our model – it is giving us the location on our model for the new data. This will cause us to search the model semantic network, the main net, until we find that part of it matching the node/edge pattern shown.

So, we are going to be involved in a search of the main net for a pattern that matches the subnet. This is termed an isomorphic search. The dictionary definition of *isomorphic* is *having the same form* or *exactly corresponding in form and relations* (Fowler & Fowler, 1989). In outline, for this simple search, this involves finding a node in the main net that matches the *cat* node in the subnet; there are three of these. We examine each one in turn to find one that has an *is* edge leading to a *second* node; there is only one match here. So, now we are in a position to commence our mental model update. Of course, this is a very simple subnet. In practice more complicated sentences with ramified clauses will lead to a much more complex subnet, but the principles remain the same.

But just identifying the corresponding subnet within the main net is not the end of the story. Let's see why. The subnet for:

- the second cat

has a distinguished instance/node *cat,* shown lower left, surrounded by dashes, in the figure following. We call this the *subject anchor.*

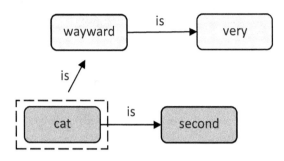

The subject anchor corresponds to what may be termed the sentence subject root. The *cat* is the thing which is *very wayward*. The upper left part of the subnet in the figure, corresponding to the phrase:

- *is very wayward*

is new data to be added to our model, but note, at the *cat* node rather than the *second* node. But again, this is not the end of the story. The subnet for the above has a distinguished node *wayward*, shown upper left in the figure following, surrounded by dashes. We call this the *object anchor*.

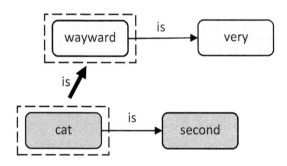

The object anchor corresponds to what may be called the sentence object root. Note that this is the attachment point *wayward* for *very wayward* rather than *very* on our mental model.

The final component of the process is the attachment edge *is*, shown bold, corresponding to the sentence main verb, so-called to distinguish it from verbs occurring in any sentence clauses. We generally separate this out from the object phrase. From the *Part I* analysis, the main verb is always *is* or *has*.

We can therefore update the main net as shown following. Note that the connection points are at the instances/nodes *cat* and *wayward*, not at the nodes *second* or *very*. The connection edge is the main verb *is*.

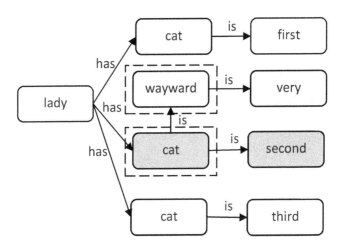

Another example

Let's review again the sentence processing we've just done by looking at another example.

If we encounter the sentence:

- *the Siamese cat is very fierce*

then basic sentence processing involves forming a subnet for the sentence subject, for example *Siamese cat (cat is Siamese)* and then another subnet for the sentence object or complement, for example *very fierce (fierce is very)*. These are shown in the following figure. As before, we separate out the main verb *is*, as shown below linking the subject and object subnets.

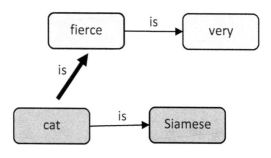

Associated with each subnet as we recall there is generally an anchor node, shown dashed in the following figure, for both the subject and object subnets. If the subject anchor were absent, we would not know whether to attach the new data to *Siamese* or *cat* when we found these on the main net. If the object anchor were absent, we would not know that the new data attachment point was *fierce* rather than *very*. As before the verb then tells us the attachment edge type, *is* or *has*.

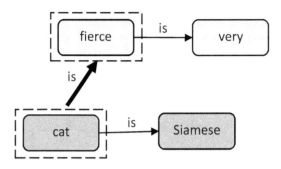

A main net search, a so-called isomorphic search, is carried out to find any subnet within the net, matching the subject subnet *Siamese cat*. This will return zero results if no subnet match if found, or one or more results if it is. As the sentence begins with the definite article *the*, there is an expectation of just one such match. We will discuss determiners such as *the* in more detail shortly.

This is the first part of the process. In practice, with most subject and object subnets, there is an anchor for each. If we remember, an anchor is a distinguished instance/node. In the example, the subject anchor is *cat* and the object anchor *fierce*. In practice, the anchors are identified when the sentence is analysed and the subnets formed during syntax and semantics analysis. *Part IV* of this book discusses software able to carry out this process. The anchors are shown for the subnets and main net in the lower and upper parts of the following figure, respectively.

We map the anchor node on the subject subnet to the corresponding node on the main net subnet, as shown in the figure. This locates the exact point on the main net where new data is to be added, that is *cat* in the example. Again, if the subject anchor were absent, then we would not know whether to attach, the *fierce is very* subnet to the node *Siamese* or *cat*. Similarly, the object anchor *fierce* enables us to attach the subject node to the correct object node, that is *fierce* rather than *very*.

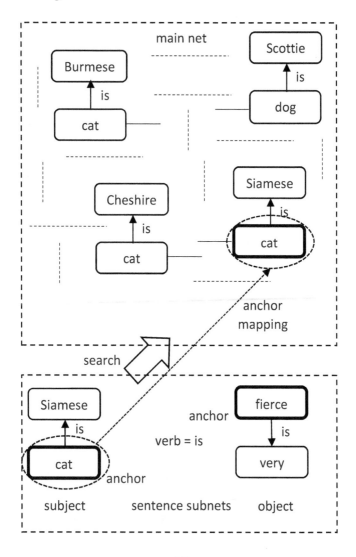

As shown in the figure following, the attachment is then carried out by adding new instances/nodes to the main net, representing *fierce* and *very* linked by a new *is* edge. Effectively, we copy the object subnet into the main net. Then finally we add a new edge representing the main verb *is* relation to link the *cat* and *fierce* nodes on the main net.

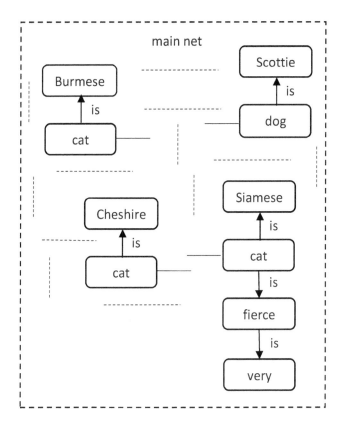

In the processes outlined, you will note that the dominant requirement is for pattern recognition, as part of the search for an isomorphic match within the main net.

The influence of determiners

Determiners generally introduce subject or object nouns, providing some information about their nature; see (Garnham, 1994) for a more detailed definition of determiners. In this section we discuss their influence on the information contributed by a sentence to the mental model.

The indefinite articles *a, an* or *another* each introduce a new instance/node to the main net. The sentence, *there is a balloon* introduces a new *balloon* instance. The article *another* may be used if there already exists an instance, for example, there is already a *balloon* instance. Attempted use of *a* or *an* when an instance is present, or *another* when absent, can be used to detect erroneous semantics.

A cardinal is also an indefinite article, introducing several instances/nodes at once. The sentence, *there are three balloons* introduces three new *balloon* instances. The word *more* may be appended to the cardinal if there already exists one or more instances, for example, *there are two more balloons.* Again, the absence of *more* when instances are present, or presence of *more* when absent, can be used to detect erroneous semantics.

Importantly, qualification of any new instance and any existing instance can be taken into consideration to validate semantics. So, if we say, *there is a red balloon* and there is already a *green balloon* then we do not need to say *another.* Similar considerations apply to *more.*

The definite article *the* may be used to refer to an existing instance/node. The sentence *the red balloon is punctured* generally identifies an existing *balloon* instance which is *red.* This is with the intention of updating the main net as previously described. But in common usage, the definite article may also be used in an indefinite sense to refer to something that does not yet exist. To deal with this, a test may be made to determine if the subject instance already exists or not. If it does not, then the definite article may be interpreted as an indefinite article, and a new instance introduced. Otherwise, only a single instance must exist, and this is referenced. Otherwise, if multiple instances are present, the reference is ambiguous, and may be used to detect erroneous semantics.

The word *each* used as a determiner can be used to references multiple instances. The sentence, *each green balloon has a string* may be used to reference several existing instances. If the instances are absent, or if there is only one, again a semantic error may be detected.

An ordinal may accompany *the* to select one instance out of a number. The sentence *The second green balloon is large* selects a specific *balloon* instance. Again, if the instance is absent, because there is only one *green balloon*, a semantic error may be flagged.

A proper noun, for example, *John*, unaccompanied by a determiner may be assumed to be preceded by an implicit *the*. Thereafter, the rule for a definite article may be followed. If *John* does not exist, then a *John* instance may be introduced. If a single *John* instance exists, then this may be referenced, otherwise the reference is ambiguous again, and a semantic error may be flagged. A quoted phrase, for example, *'Transport for London'*, or an abbreviation, for example, *TFL*, unaccompanied by a determiner, may be treated as a proper noun and made to follow the same rules.

The previous considerations show that in practice, both subject and object subnets searches of the main net are always needed, whether these represent new data (associated with indefinite articles e.g. *a*), or existing data (associated with definite articles e.g. *the*). With new data, checks are needed for erroneous semantics, for example, not using *another* or *more* when necessary. With existing data, checks are needed for existence, or for use of *the* instead of *each*, and so on.

An anchor is unrequired for sentences such as *count each Siamese cat*, as we are just counting pattern occurrences, or declarations such as *there is a Siamese cat* as we are just adding new unanchored data. An anchor is required for sentences such as *viewing the Siamese cat*, dealt with in more detail later, to precisely locate the topic tree.

Description of a triangle

Just to round things off and to illustrate typical determiner usage, here is a description of a triangle which, with the *AI Dialog* software demonstrator, is able to generate a corresponding mental model.

- *a triangle has an ab side, a bc side and a ca side*
- *each side is a straight line*
- *the triangle has an abc angle, a bca angle and a cab angle*
- *the ab side and the bc side each shares the abc angle*
- *the bc side and the ca side each shares the bca angle*
- *the ca side and the ab side each shares the cab angle*

Querying our mental model

Moving on now, let's see how we can query our mental model. Suppose we encounter the query sentence:

- *the lady has how many cats?*

How can we manage to create a meaningful reply to this?

Again, the first step is to reduce the sentence to *is* and *has* expressions alone. The analysis of this sentence is quite brief really, but nevertheless sufficient for our purposes:

> • *the lady has how many cats*
> - *lady has cat*

We must frankly admit that here there is also some metadata not entirely represented in the *is-has* analysis, indicating that this is a query. The corresponding subnet is shown following. In theory, we could put it into a 'count' context.

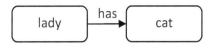

We can then perform another isomorphic search of our mental model main net to find any pattern that matches the query sentence subnet pattern. As we can see to the left in the figure following, we get three matches from the search, labelled (1), (2) and (3). So, we can use this result to reply to the query:

> • *the lady has how many cats*

with:

• the lady has three cats

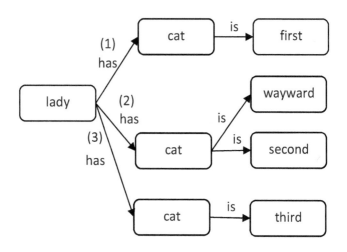

Isomorphic subnet searching

We can see from this example that both model updates and model queries involve searching an established mental model represented by a main net, for location data. Searches are always performed by building a subnet from the update or query sentence and searching the net for any matching subnets; an isomorphic subnet search. The update subnet may reference potentially existing and new components whilst the query subnet references existing components only. As previously commented both potentially existing and potentially new subnet data is generally searched for, the latter being required for sentence semantics validity checks.

We can contrast the isomorphic subnet search which is essentially a pattern recognition search with an Aristotelian logic search. The logic search is implicit within the pattern search.

As an example, implicit in *the blue balloon has a long string*, with semantic subnet of A following, is the main net search of the net B following, for the *blue balloon*. This means locating *balloon* instances and determining if they have the *blue* property. But as we are seeing, this is not done using logic, but by performing an isomorphic subnet search. If just one *blue balloon* subnet is found then *long string* is associated with it, otherwise if more than one is found, the sentence is ambiguous. C following shows the result on the main net. A similar search is needed for an explicit query, using an imperative such as *count each blue balloon,* to which the response would be *there is one blue balloon.*

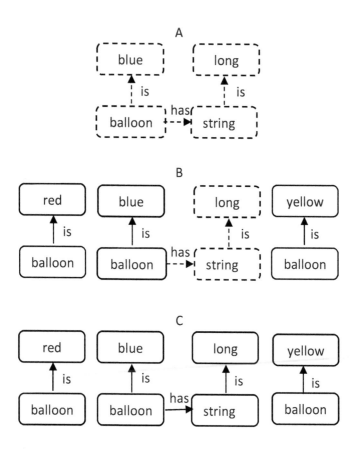

Unknown references

We can perform a search using so-called unknown references. Often words like *thing* or *person* can be used to reference unknown instances/nodes. The sentence *list each thing that Jack has* involves finding the *Jack* instance and listing any unknown *thing*, related to it by *has*. If there is more than one *Jack*, then the sentence is ambiguous. Subnet *A* following is derived from the example. The instances *rope*, *pail* and *spade* of the net *B*, all map to unknown reference *thing* and we can respond with *a rope, a pail,* and *a spade.* An unknown reference is rather like a 'wild card', it will match anything, provided that the remainder of the subnet of which it is a part also finds a match.

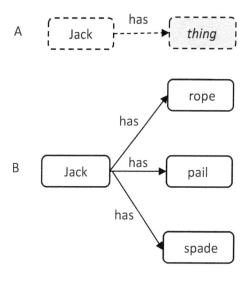

A more complex query

Let's now have a look at a rather more complex query on our model involving again unknown references. Suppose we encounter the sentences:

> • *Jack, Cole, and Humpty each likes Jill*

and then:

> • *Jill likes Jack and Humpty*

This is illustrated in the figure following.

After the sentence:

• *Jack, Cole, and Humpty each likes Jill*

our model main net, from *Part I*, is as shown following.

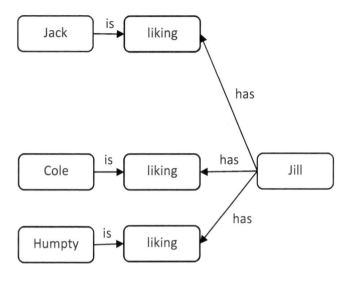

After the subsequent sentence:

• *Jill likes Jack and Humpty*

our model is augmented with data as shown following. The new data is added into the right place using the isomorphic search and anchor techniques described earlier.

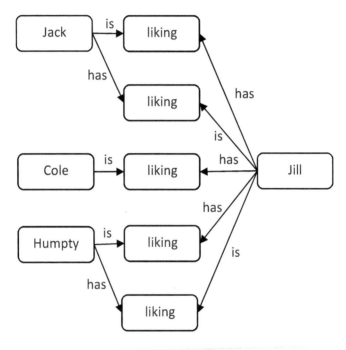

Suppose we then encounter the query sentence:

- *list each person that likes Jill, that Jill likes*

How can we tackle this and derive an answer to it?

We begin as always by reducing the sentence to *is-has* expressions:

- *list each person that likes Jill, that Jill likes*
    - *Jill is liking*
    - *person has liking (liking of person)*
    - *person is liking*
    - *Jill has liking (liking of Jill)*

and building the corresponding sentence subnet shown following.

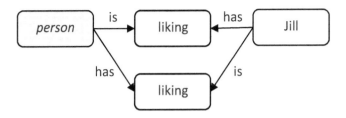

As previously noted, in this situation the instance/node *person* is special. When we start to search the main net, the node *person* is allowed to match anything. As previously mentioned, it's like a 'wild card'. Not only that, but the actual nodes that *person* matches during the search, are of interest, and we need to know about them and to record them.

So, the previous subnet has the matches shown outlined in the net following.

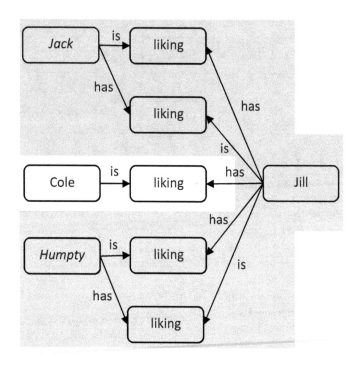

From these, *person* matches *Jack* and *Humpty*, shown italicised in the diagram, but <u>not</u> *Cole*. So, we are able to reply to the query:

> • *list each person that likes Jill, that Jill likes*
> with:
> • *Jack and Humpty*

as *person* matches these.

An assertion

In just one final aspect of mental model queries, let's have a look at an assertion example. Suppose we have an assertion, such as:

- *Cole likes Jill!*

and we need to determine its truth or otherwise. We again begin by reducing the assertion to *is/has* expressions.

- *Cole likes Jill*
  - *Cole is liking*
  - *Jill has liking (liking of Jill)*

Then we form the subnet from this, as shown following:.

We search the main net with this subnet, and if we find the match as shown following, we answer *true*, otherwise we answer *false*.

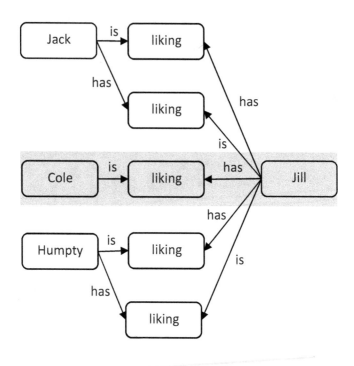

Definitions, instances, and meanings

In *Part I* we started to touch upon definitions and instances when we looked at the difference in sense between *X is Y* and *X is a Y* i.e., when a determiner follows the *is* verb. We are now going to look at definitions and instances in greater detail. We are then going to look at a related concept and that is *meaning*, in fact, examining the meaning of *meaning*.

Definitions

We are used to the idea of definitions of things appearing in a dictionary or encyclopedia. However, a key aspect of a definition in the sense that we use it here, is that it tends to be associated with a noun. Let's begin with an example of a definition of a *doctor*. We might encounter a sentence like this: *every doctor: is caring; is skilled; has a medical degree* which we can analyse as follows.

> • *every doctor: is caring; is skilled; has a medical degree*
>> - *a doctor is caring*
>> - *a doctor is skilled*
>> - *a doctor has a degree*
>> - *the degree is medical*

The corresponding semantic network for this definition is shown following. Note the use of a *definition context* to contain the detailed definition of a doctor. This is to separate out the definition from other semantic networks, so that the logic for one does not get mixed up with the logic for the other e.g., during the isomorphic searches. How the definition itself and the declaration of the definition *doctor has definition* are linked is touched upon in the later section *Contexts and network nodes*.

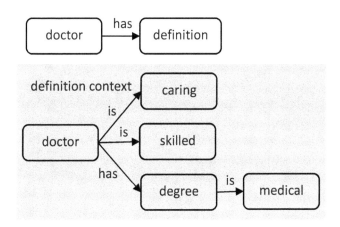

The example here shows definition creation triggered by

using a sentence beginning with *every* i.e. *every doctor*. We could if we wished qualify the subject as in *every doctor of medicine*. Also, once created, we could add further attributes, for example, *every doctor shares the common code of medical ethics*.

Instances

Now looking at an instance creation example. Suppose we encounter the sentence:

• *Jack is a doctor*

An initial subnet for this sentence is shown following.

But if a definition of a *doctor* exists, when we encounter the sentence, we can automatically augment our mental model as shown in the net following, by copying data from the definition context subnet.

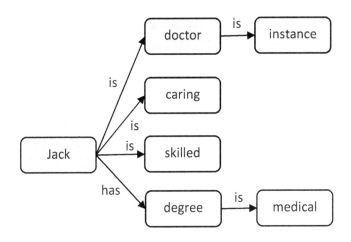

As a variation, we could say:

• *Jack is a doctor of medicine*

With the subnet shown in *A* following. Then we would have to match with a modified definition as shown in *B* following.

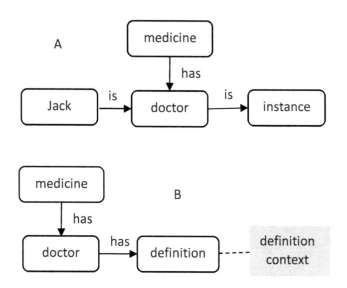

Nested definitions

Definitions may be nested, with one definition appearing inside another. So as part of the doctor *definition*, we may have the sentence:

• *a doctor is a professional*

as shown in the subnet following. You will recognise this sort of mechanism appearing in dictionary definitions of words. Almost always these define words in terms of other words. If you do not understand these latter then you use the dictionary again to check their definitions in turn, and so on.

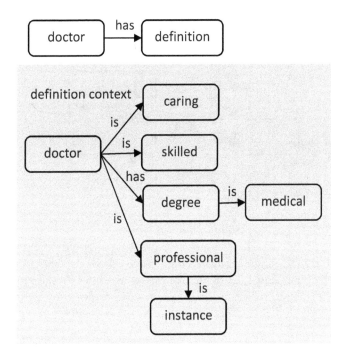

And then we can have a definition of a *professional*:

- *every professional: is salaried; is respected*
    - *a professional is salaried*
    - *a professional is respected*

and so on, as shown in the subnet following:

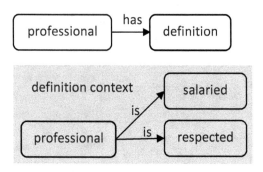

So, when we encounter:

• *Jack is a doctor*

a double augmentation takes place, firstly of the *doctor* attributes and then of the *professional* attributes as shown in the subnet following.

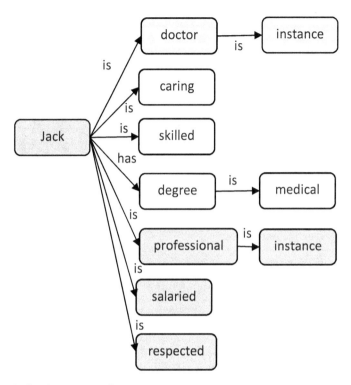

A further example

Here is a further example of nested definitions. In the sentence *every cat: has a tail and whiskers; is a quadruped,* the phrase *is a quadruped* within the definition creates a *quadruped* instance.

We may then have a further definition that *every quadruped: has a left front leg, a right front leg, a left back leg, and a right back leg.*

If we then encounter the sentence *Felix is a cat,* the result is shown following in *A, B* and *C.* The first definition causes *whiskers, tail,* and *quadruped* to be added to *Felix.* Then the nested definition, caused by the *quadruped* instance, adds *legs.*

In practice, we may nest definitions to any depth.

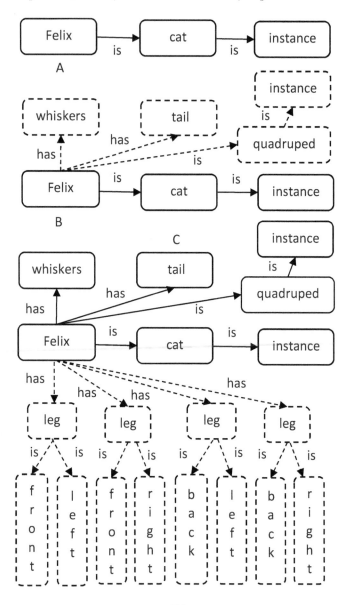

Meanings

A key aspect of the word *meaning* in the sense we are about to use it here, is that it is generally associated with non-nouns, and in fact mostly adjectives, adverbs, prepositions, and participles. Otherwise, we handle meanings in pretty much the same way as definitions. Let's give an example using the participle *climbing*. We would like to have a description of what *climbing* involves, what is it all about i.e., what is the meaning of *climbing* or *to climb*? As just mentioned, you will observe in what follows substantial overlap with the handling of definitions.

We might say: *climbing* means *going up*; *climbing* is an *activity*; *hills, mountains, and ladders* are all *climbable*. With the word *climbable* here, we are really saying that it is sensible to use the concept of *climbing* in regard to *hills, mountains,* and *ladders,* not that in specific cases they are necessarily actually *climbable*. These assertions are then reflected in the following description of the meaning of *climbing,* which is then followed by the corresponding semantic network. Again, in this we have a separate context for the meaning description, just as with a definition.

> • *climbing is going up*
>   - *going is up*
> • *climbing is an activity*
>   - *activity is instance*
> • *hill has climbing*
>   - *hill is every*
> • *mountain has climbing*
>   - *mountain is every*
> • *ladder has climbing*
>   - *ladder is every*

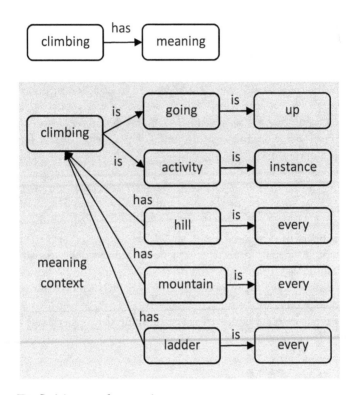

Definition and meaning notes

We pause here to mention one or two technical aspects of definitions and meanings. Definition representations in semantic networks are discussed by Sowa (Sowa, 1992) but the approach here differs. A definition or meaning here is similar to that of a dictionary word, but in the software, implementation is rationalised to aid computation. There are also parallels with class definitions within object-oriented programming (OOP) languages (Wegner, 1987). A definition or meaning here is limited to:

- *is-set* memberships, for example, *someone who is caring;* this *definition* implicitly includes all general verbs, for example, *someone who shares the code of ethics,* since this is equivalent to *someone who is sharing the code of ethics*
- *has-set* memberships, for example, *someone who has a medical degree*
- *instance* references, for example, *someone who is a person*

With object-oriented class data comparisons, as in, for example, the programming language C# (Liberty, 2005), the first two items resemble normal data definitions, and the last item resembles an object instantiation definition.

The previous examples have implied a permanence of additions when an instance results in the consulting of a definition. However, it is accepted that in many circumstances it may be desirable to only add this data transiently as part of a thought process directed towards establishing a logical conclusion; a 'temporary' context.

A final point is that almost everything i.e. almost every instance/node has an underlying definition or meaning, whether such a definition or meaning is explicitly present on the mental model or not.

Contexts and network nodes

We have seen earlier, in respect of verb tenses and reported speech in *Part I*, and definitions, and meanings, in this *Part,* a need for what we might term a *context* facility. We will also see a need when handling sequences of events as described later on in this section. A context here is a region that is capable of containing a whole semantic sub-network, and effectively providing some degree of isolation for it from the main network. In some situations we need to be able to manipulate the internal content this sub-network, but in other situations we need to treat the whole sub-network as if it were a single entity. We need to have separation of this sub-network from other parts of the network, so that the two do not get mixed up especially during isomorphic searches.

The approach chosen here, although it is probably not the only one, is via that of the network node. So far we have seen that nodes have always been used to represent named instances of something, or someone, or some action e.g., *balloon, station, hill, Jack, Jill, climbing, liking,* and so on. Occasionally, a node has represented an extended name e.g., *London Underground* or a reported speech phrase e.g., *Jill will carry the pail.* We now extend the concept of what a node is able to represent, to allow it to represent a whole semantic sub-network.

Let us now revisit each of those aspects of networks requiring a context facility to see how this concept enables such a facility to be implemented.

Verb tenses

In the following figure we see the semantic network representing a sentence we encountered earlier in *Part I*: *the girl who won the race will receive (get) a prize.* The network has two contexts, one containing the subnet for *the girl who won the race* – a past context, and one containing the subnet for *the girl will get a prize* – a future context. We see from the network that the past context becomes the content of a *past node*. We can then use this node in a simple two node subnet representing the phrase *the past node is past* to label the subnet content of the context as taking part in the past. Similarly, the future context becomes the content of a *future node* and again we use the node network representing *the future node is future* to label the context content as in the future.

We suggest there are ambiguities surrounding adjectives and similar parts of speech in the situation of tenses. In adjective strings preceding nouns, tense information is absent, so for example, in the phrase *will get a valuable prize,* although we know *get* is in the future, we do not know if *prize* is *valuable* is in the past, present or future.

There remain many unanswered questions in this area.

A notable point is that the *girl* node is referred to in both the past and future contexts. Any technical difficulty that might arise in a software implementation of an item appearing to exist in two places at once, may be avoided by using so-called references (effectively pointers) to the item from each context, rather than placing the item itself there. This is a common facility available in contemporary software languages (Walmsley, 1997).

We note that semantic networks only ever represent case imperfect expressions e.g., *Jack is climbing the hill.* But the sentence from which a particular representation was derived may have been case perfect e.g., *Jack climbs the hill.* During sentence synthesis from semantic networks, as discussed later in the section *Sentence synthesis*, if there is ever a need to correctly regenerate case perfect, then considerations of contexts and network nodes help us to do so.

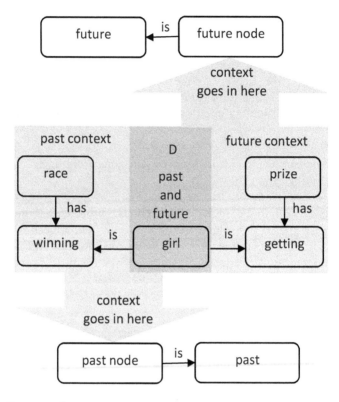

Reported speech or thoughts

This is another earlier topic that we are now going to revisit in the situation of contexts and network nodes. In an earlier analysis in *Part I* of reported speech exemplified by the sentence *Jack says 'Jill will carry the pail'*, we kept the analysis of *Jill will carry the pail* separate and unconnected with the analysis of *Jack says 'Jill will carry the pail'* as shown in the following network. Note that the subnet of *Jill will carry the pail* is in the future context.

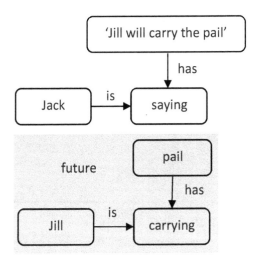

The following semantic network completes the analysis by making use of contexts and network nodes. Firstly, the subnet represented by *Jill will carry the pail*, which is in the future context, is loaded into a *future node*. A simple two node network then enables us to label the node as representing a future context. This network in turn is loaded into a *saying* node. The latter is used in a three node network representing *Jack says 'Jill will carry the pail'*.

A point this brings out is that not only can we load a whole network into a network node, but we can then use that node in another network, which is in turn loaded into another network node, in turn used in another network, and so on to any depth we need.

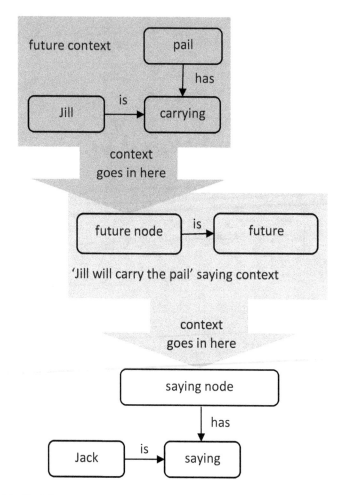

Definitions

Again we revisit an earlier topic in the situation of contexts and network nodes. In a definition we had a need to link the definition itself with the declaration of the definition e.g., *doctor has definition*, in the earlier *doctor* example. Again this is achievable using a network node. The following semantic network illustrates how. The *definition context* containing the definition semantic network is loaded into the *definition* node.

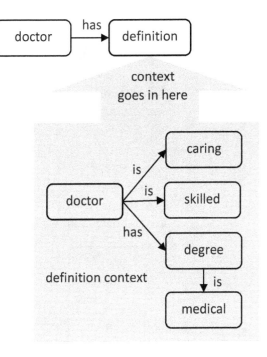

Sequences of events

Let's now consider some sentences representing sequences of events. This is something quite new and we need the facilities of contexts and network nodes to be able to represent them. We will be having another look here too at distinguishing between case perfect and case imperfect sentences, helping us to distinguish, if we need to, between case perfect as in:

* *Jack climbs up the hill*

and case imperfect as in:

• *Jack is climbing up the hill*

Suppose we have some sentences describing a sequence of events like this, and analysed as shown:

• *event B is after event A*
  - *event A has after*
  - *event B is after*
• *event C is after event B*
  - *event B has after*
  - *event C is after*

The semantic network is shown following.

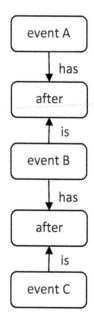

The following set of sentences could represent the events *A*, *B* and *C*.

- *Jack climbs up the hill (event A)*
- *next, Jack fills the pail (event B)*
- *next, Jack climbs down the hill (event C)*

By using contexts and network nodes we can therefore arrive at the following semantic network representing the event sequence described.

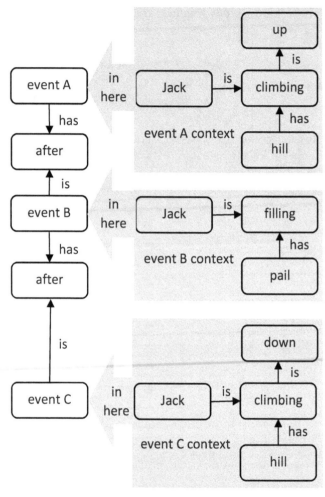

Suppose now that we have another activity taking place at the same time as one of *Jack's* activities as reflected in the following sentences.

- *Jack climbs up the hill (event A)*
- *next, Jack fills the pail (event B)*

- *Jill watches Jack (event B')*
- *next, Jack climbs down the hill (event C)*

Contexts and network nodes give the following network.

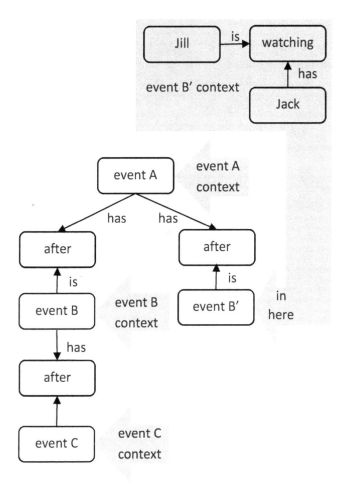

This brings out a number of points. The sentiment of event

A i.e. *Jack climbs up the hill* is case perfect as the implication is that the event is terminated by event *B* i.e. *next, Jack fills the pail*. Similarly with event *B* terminated by event *C* i.e. *next, Jack climbs down the hill*. However, the sentiment of event *B'* i.e. *Jill watches Jack* is case imperfect as we are never told when *Jill* stops *watching Jack*. Note that we cannot bundle *Jack fills the pail* into the same context *as Jill watches Jack* as the former is terminated by *next, Jack climbs down the hill*, whilst the latter remains unterminated.

Sequences of events and their representation on a semantic network is quite a complex topic, and we have only scratched the surface of the topic here, but hopefully sufficiently to give some idea of the potential.

Further possible node content

To review a few things, we have seen that nodes can contain words or quoted text strings or very occasionally nothing at all i.e. so-called anonymous or null nodes. We have seen latterly that nodes can contain whole semantic networks. But there is also the potential to allow nodes to contain even further data types e.g., blocks of text, files, or images, and so on. In this treatise we limit ourselves to just the types of data previously described, but acknowledge the potential to extend to these further data types.

Isomorphic subnet searching

The presence of network nodes containing semantic network contexts naturally adds complications to the isomorphic subnet searches discussed earlier. Let's have a look at a past tense example. Suppose we have the question *how often did Jack climb?* The analysis of this is shown in the upper part of the following diagram. We see that *Jack is climbing* is loaded into *past node'*. This node is then made part of the two node network *past node' is past*.

The isomorphic search of the main net requires two stages. In the first stage we search for *something is past* where *something* is a wild card network node. The main net example in the figure would result in matches with *past node 1* and *past node 2*. The other two network nodes *future node* and *present node* would not qualify. At this point we have the second stage, to access the network contained in each of *past node 1* and *past node 2* and carry out an isomorphic subnet search for the semantic network contained in *past node'*.

This is a very simple example and in practice the search may be quite ramified if, for example network nodes contain networks containing other network nodes, as in the earlier reported speech example.

Further discussion of this topic again lies beyond the remit of this particular text.

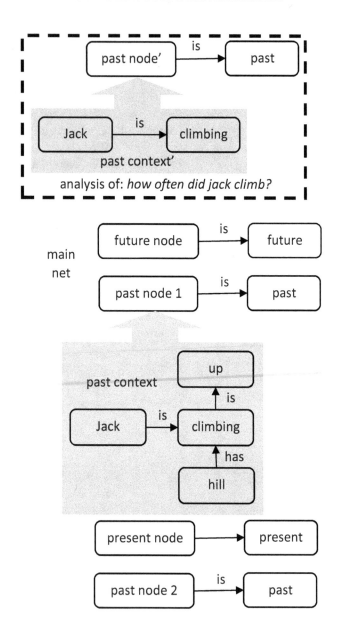

analysis of: *how often did jack climb?*

main net

past context

Instance references across contexts

We saw with the earlier verb tense example of *the girl who won the race will receive a prize* that the *girl* instance can appear in two contexts, one associated with the past and one with the future. There are two problems we need to look at here.

The first is how can any software AI technology recognise that the two *girl* references represent the same *girl* instance. The answer lies in the sentence context. In the example given, the deduction is easy because the two contexts are built from one common *girl* reference in one sentence. A more complicated case would be represented by two sentences e.g. *Jack climbed the hill* and then later *Jack will climb the same hill again*. We can see that with the right sentence semantics it is possible for an AI system to arrive at the correct conclusion.

A purely software technical issue arising with contexts is how are multiple instance references in multiple contexts recognised as being associated with the same instance. One possible method is to make use of an instance integer. These have been mentioned earlier in the section *The semantic network mental model, Instances* with different *cat* instances being distinguished by *cat(1), cat(2), cat(3)* and so on. The following diagram of semantic network contexts illustrates the principle.

With the sentence *the girl who won the race will get a prize*, shown in the upper two contexts, the *girl* is common, shown by the *girl(1)* instance references, whilst *race(1), winning(1), prize(1)* and *getting(1)* have only one instance reference each.

With the sentences *Jack climbed the hill* and *Jack will climb another hill, Jack* is the same in each of the lower contexts shown by *Jack(1)* in each. The *climbing* is a different *climbing* in each, and would be even if the same *hill* was involved, shown by *climbing(1)* and *climbing(2)*. The hill is different in each, shown by *hill(1)* and *hill(2)*. Hopefully this brief description has given you some flavour of the possible approach.

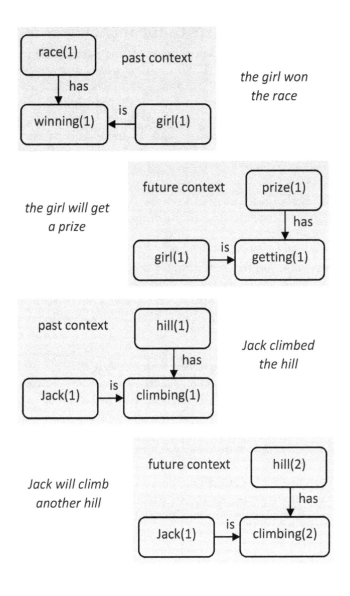

Viewing just parts of the mental model

Although the mental model examples you have already seen have been quite simple, you can appreciate that practical mental models representing complex real world organisations could become quite large and ramified, which could either result in long search times for topics, or ambiguities where the same semantic term has been used in different contexts to refer to different things. Here we examine a theory for viewing and manipulating just part of the mental model, whilst ignoring the rest. We can refer to this process as *localisation*. Let's just look at a few sentences illustrating manipulation of the mental model in this respect.

The sentence *two ladies each has a dog, a cat and a budgie* adds two *ladies*, *dogs*, *cats* and *budgies* to the semantic network example following. A subsequent sentence *the cat has two toys* is ambiguous because we do not know if it is the *cat* belonging to the *first* or *second lady*. We could clarify this by saying *the cat of the second lady has two toys*. Alternatively, as shown in the lower network part, we may change our view of the mental model by saying *viewing (or considering or looking at) the second lady*. We can now unambiguously say *the cat has two toys* because the *cat* can be unambiguously identified as that belonging to the *second lady*. We may shift our view still further with *viewing (or considering or looking at) the cat* and then *viewing (or considering) the first toy*. We may move backwards from the point of view of the *toy* to the *cat*, with *leaving the first toy* or *leaving the previous*. We may shift to considering the whole mental model or main net again by saying *viewing (or considering or looking at) the whole*. The dashed lines on the lower example illustrate these possibilities.

Although a view shifts our primary consideration to just one part of the model or net, there is no reason why more global earlier views cannot still be referenced if there is no ambiguity. So, in the example, although we may be viewing *the first toy,* we can still sensibly refer to *cat,* without qualification, in the previous view, but not sensibly refer to just *lady* in the even earlier view; we would have to say, *second lady.*

You will appreciate that sentences containing forms of words causing this type of mental view shift are quite common, especially in technical documents.

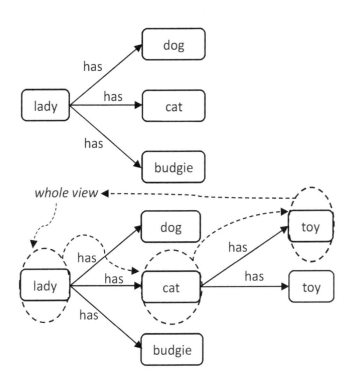

Here is another rather more complex example. Suppose we have part of an engineering specification, reflected in the following sentences, which are then followed by the corresponding semantic network.

- *a control-centre has two control-rooms*
- *the first room is main*
- *the second room is standby*
- *viewing the first room*
  - we use this to view only part of the mental model i.e., the *first room* – the viewing process is shown by dashed lines on the network following
- *the room has a supervisory desk and an incident desk*
  - we now only need to say *room* not *first* or *second room*
- *viewing the supervisory desk*
  - now we can view the *supervisory desk* only, using *viewing* ... again – the process is once more shown by dashed lines on the network
- *the desk has a telephone and two screens*
  - again, we now only need to say *desk*
- *the centre has air-conditioning*
  - however, we can still refer to an earlier topic e.g., *centre* if it can be unambiguously identified – see the *whole view* on the network
- *leaving the supervisory desk*
  - we can go back a step like this
- *leaving the previous*
  - or go back a further step like this, or at any time we can dismiss all views and view globally using *viewing the whole* – again see the *whole view* on the network

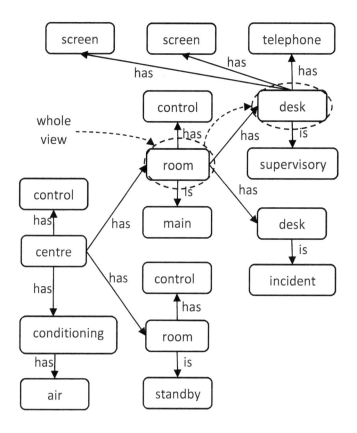

View theory

Looking now briefly at some of the theory behind views. Each viewpoint is effectively the root of a tree. During sentence processing, when we perform the isomorphic search for a sentence subnet, we start at this root. If the search fails, we try an earlier root, and so on.

This process of searching from a root, and then if the search fails, searching from an earlier root, is exemplified by 1 – 5 in the following figure. This process actually mirrors processes used in the scoping of variables in contemporary software languages (Kernighan & Ritchie, 1988). But we suggest they also reflect our own thought processes, where we localise our consideration to just one part of a complex topic. Localisation is also similar to semantic network partitioning (Hendrix, 1975) but here partitioning is implicit rather than explicit.

This is not the only approach possible to localisation. Another involves the use of the network node contexts previously described. For example each control-room could be represented by a separate context, and the desks as contexts nested within these contexts and so on. However further detailed discussion of this topic again lies beyond the scope of this particular text.

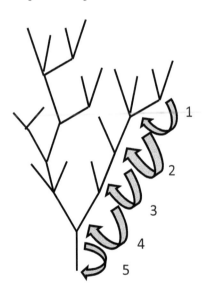

Sentence synthesis

So far our attention has been mainly concentrated on input

sentence analysis and augmenting our mental model from input sentence semantic content. We are now going to have a look at synthesising entirely new sentences from the model. We may need to do this in response to a request such as *describe Jack,* having previously learned that *Jack is a doctor.*

Generally, a sentence may be synthesised by traversing its semantic subnet, and building component phrases. But there are complications. This is because as previously discussed, particularly in *Part I, Loss of information,* many differing grammatical forms for a phrase or sentence may actually have exactly the same subnet. For example, all the following sentences:

> • *Jack is climbing the hill*
>> - *(Jack* stressed, then *hill* stressed)
> • *The hill is being climbed by Jack*
>> - *(hill* stressed, then *climbing* stressed)
> • *The climbing of the hill is by Jack*
>> - *(climbing* stressed, then *hill* stressed)
> • *The climbing by Jack is of the hill*
>> - *(climbing* stressed then *Jack* stressed)

have the same semantic subnet as shown following:

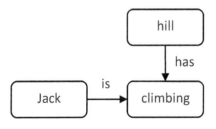

As these examples demonstrate, we have these differing

grammatical forms so that we can stress certain topics in the sentence which emotionally we feel are important. As we can see, in the first it is *Jack*, in the second the *hill*, in the third the *climbing* and in the fourth the *climbing by Jack*.

This leads to the interesting conclusion that it appears pretty well impossible to synthesise a sentence from a semantic subnet that does not stress something, whether we consciously wish it to or not. This is an inevitable consequence of the serial nature of sentence words; every word in the sentence cannot occupy the same position, for example, the first or last word, or any other position we choose in the sentence. Yet every word position, particularly the first few and last few, cause us to consciously or unconsciously attach a particular level of importance to the topic the word represents.

But stepping around this issue, suppose we do want to synthesise a sentence using a particular grammatical form reflecting a sentence topic or topics we regard as significant, how do we achieve this aim?

One method makes use of the anchor concept again, which we previously touched upon in the situation of augmenting the mental model with information from an analysed sentence in the section on *Updating our mental model*. For this to work we need to have primary, secondary and possibly further anchors in descending order of significance, although in practice, anchors beyond primary and secondary become less likely. Each anchor is associated with a sentence topic which we regard as important. The primary anchor is associated with the most important topic, the secondary anchor, the next most important topic, and so on. The anchors will then govern the grammatical form of a synthesised sentence. They do this by guiding the traversal path along the subnet as the sentence is synthesised.

To see how this works, let's go back to the original example shown following:

> • *Jack is climbing the hill*
> > - (*Jack* primary, *climbing* secondary)
> • *The hill is being climbed by Jack*
> > - (*hill* primary, *climbing* secondary)
> • *The climbing of the hill is by Jack*
> > - (*climbing* primary, *hill* secondary)
> • *The climbing by Jack is of the hill*
> > - (*climbing* primary, *Jack* secondary)

In *A*, *B*, *C*, and *D* of the following subnet, we see for each of the previous variations respectively, the primary anchor shown with the boldest outline, followed by the secondary anchor, with a less bold outline, and so on. A sentence synthesising algorithm is then able to traverse the subnet, from the primary anchor position onwards, being steered along a preferential path by the secondary and possibly tertiary anchors, and so on.

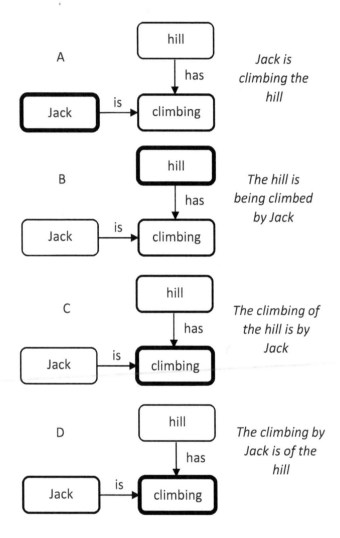

A — Jack is climbing the hill

B — The hill is being climbed by Jack

C — The climbing of the hill is by Jack

D — The climbing by Jack is of the hill

Without going into full detail of the subnet traversal algorithm for synthesising a sentence, we can look at one or two basic rules. Going forwards via a *has* edge i.e., following the directional arrow, we synthesise *has* in the sentence.

Going backwards via a *has* edge i.e., against the directional arrow, we tend to get *of*, but, in common parlance, *of* is suppressed unless the previous instance/node is a participle. Going forwards via an *is* edge, we synthesise *is* in the sentence. Going backwards via an *is* edge, we get *is by*, if the previous instance/node is a participle, or *of*, if it is not. Notably, if we ever backtrack through a node, we begin to synthesise a clause.

Using these rules and starting at the node with most stress we get, for subnet *A* above:

- *Jack is climbing (of) the hill*

For subnet *C* we get:

- *the climbing of the hill is by Jack*

Note the clause *of the hill* created by backtracking via the *climbing* node in subnet *C*.

We might want to keep the stress on *climbing* but stress *Jack* more and the *hill* less. These stresses are shown for subnet *D*, and result in the sentence:

- *the climbing by Jack is of the hill*

Again, the clause *by Jack* results from backtracking via *climbing*. Note that interestingly *of* is not suppressed in this particular grammatical construction.

We can only speculate whether the mechanisms described here parallel our own thought processes. It is possible that we really do mentally synthesise a sentence from underlying semantic data, choosing aspects of that data we wish to emphasise based on our perceived order of importance of that emphasis. So if we feel *climbing* is the most important aspect, closely followed by *hill*, then perhaps our mental anchor order really is as shown in the previous net *C*, and so on. Who knows?

Describe

We conclude this section by having a brief look at synthesising a whole sequence of sentences associated with describing something. In practice, similar mechanisms to those mentioned earlier for views and localisation on our mental model are involved when we are asked to describe something.

The reason for this is that when we give a good, well-organised description of something, we tend to move progressively from the general to the more specific. This corresponds to going up our mental model tree as in 1 – 8 of the following diagram. This movement up the tree will be recognised as being associated with progressive view selection.

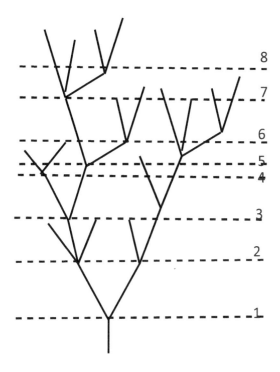

To move on to a concrete example, suppose we encounter the sentence:

• *describe Jack*

and suppose we have previously been informed that *Jack is a doctor*, coupled with an existing definition of a *doctor*, resulting in the subnet following. We have already encountered this subnet in the earlier section on *Definitions, instances, and meanings*.

The subnet traversal algorithm begins at the node *Jack* labelled 1, and then traverses the tree following the nodes labelled 2 – 7 in order.

To do this, the algorithm makes successive use the previously described *view* function on each tree branch.

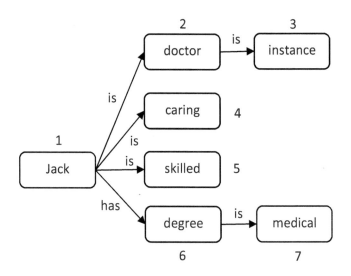

The result is shown below:

- *there is just one Jack*
- *viewing Jack*
- *Jack is a doctor, caring and skilled*
- *Jack has a degree*
- *viewing the degree*
- *the degree is medical*
- *leaving the degree*
- *leaving Jack*

Supporting the traversal algorithm is a syntactic manipulation algorithm which merges successive *is* expressions such as *Jack is a doctor, Jack is caring,* and *Jack is skilled* into a sentence such as *Jack is a doctor, caring and skilled.*

Translation

Just one further topic before we conclude this section. There is no reason why sentence synthesis from a network representing a mental model should be in the same language as that used to build the model; it could be in a different language. There would be a minimum need to look up the target language words corresponding to the node names. There would also be a need to consider other factors such as gender matching and differing word order. Nevertheless, sentence synthesis from a network does provide a key starting point for language translation. Such translation could be carried out on a sentence-by-sentence basis using the subnet derived from each sentence, or on a whole discourse basis using the entire model network.

Conclusion

This has been only a very brief overview of sentence synthesis, together with a very simple example of its use. Sentence synthesis from a network is, in reality, a very big topic in its own right.

Data structure of the mental model

Directed graph data structure

We pause here to consider the underlying data structure of the mental model. The semantic network in general is what is termed a directed graph data structure (Goodrich & Tamassia, 2015). It consists of nodes (sometimes referred to as vertices) and directed edges between nodes, shown following.

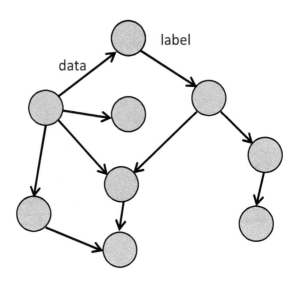

In the simplest case, each node, as we have seen, carries a label, which is generally a single English sentence word, but occasionally a quoted phrase. Each edge, in addition to its direction carries data. This is always *is* or *has*.

But we have seen previously in the section *Contexts and network nodes*, that in order to handle verb tenses other than the present, reported speech or thoughts, definitions, and sequences of events, we need to allow nodes to contain whole semantic networks, which we have termed contexts.

Tree data structure

We can contrast the directed graph data structure with that of a tree data structure shown following.

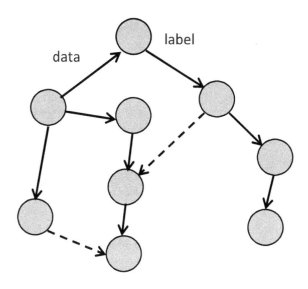

With a tree data structure, we can only ever have one edge going into a node, and the edges shown dashed are prohibited. The type of semantic network we have been discussing so far cannot be accommodated by a tree data structure because, at the very least, the common occurrence of nodes with both *is* and *has* edges going into them, as shown in the following example of a network representing *Jack is climbing the hill.*

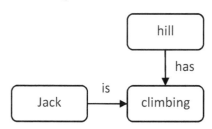

This means that algorithms used to process the mental model

must be able to handle directed graphs rather than just trees.

Isomorphic subgraph search

As we have seen, a particular requirement of the graph handling software is an ability to perform a search to find subnet matches in the mental model main net. As previously mentioned, this is termed an isomorphic subgraph search for matches within a main graph, as illustrated in the figure following. There are a number of standard algorithms for carrying out this process, but generally it is computationally expensive (Wikipedia, 2023). The additional complication is that our nodes are allowed to contain what are effectively further main graphs (contexts) posing an extended need to carry out isomorphic subgraph searches on these.

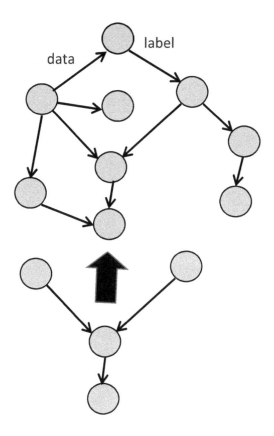

Subgraph search time

Let's have a look at the performance aspects of the subgraph search. Suppose we have a sentence:

> • *the lady's very fierce Siamese cat is happy*

with the following semantic subnet representing the subject only i.e., *the lady's very fierce Siamese cat.*

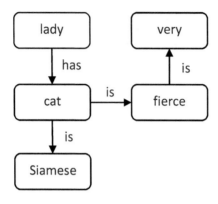

There are 5 nodes in this subject representing *lady, very, fierce, Siamese* and *cat*. One of the tasks we need to perform is to search the main net for any instances of the illustrated subnet.

Let's suppose there are 10 instances of each of the 5 nodes, some of which are parts of instances of the illustrated subnet and some of which are associated with other subject, or object subnets associated with sentences such as *another lady has three Burmese cats,* or *a man has two very fierce bulldogs* and so on.

A simple-minded brute force approach to this task is to search the main net for every instance of a *lady* node, combined with every instance of a *very* node, combined with ever instance of a *fierce* node, and so on, for the *lady, very, fierce, Siamese* and *cat* nodes.

For every combination, we then look at the edges connecting the nodes, for correspondence with the edge types shown in the illustrated subnet. Whenever this condition is satisfied then we have found an isomorphic subnet within the main net.

The number of combinations to be searched will be recognised to be:

- 10 (*lady*) x 10 (*very*) x 10 (*fierce*) x 10 (*Siamese*) x 10 (*cat*) = 100.000 combinations

We can therefore work out a general formula for the number of combinations to be searched, for an average of N instances of each subject node, and s for the number of subject node types as:

- combinations = N^s or N to the power of s

Clearly, we are going to end up with some pretty big numbers for larger numbers of instance nodes. For example, if there are an average of 100 *lady* nodes and 100 *very* nodes and so on for *lady*, *very*, *fierce*, *Siamese* and *cat*, we end up with:

- combinations = 100^5 = 10,000,000,000 or 10 billion

This number of combinations to work through in a reasonable amount of time is going to be challenging to do even for contemporary high performance computer processors.

Subgraph search time mitigation

There are a variety of ways of mitigating the subgraph search time. Suppose out of the N nodes previously mentioned they are evenly distributed between two self-contained contexts such that any occurrences of the subgraph are wholly contained within a context i.e., they do not overlap across two contexts. The number of combinations to be checked in each context is given by:

- combinations = $(100/2)^5$ = 312,000,500, or for

both contexts, the above x 2 = 624,001,000

The performance improvement factor is as follows:

- factor = $10,000,000,000/624,001,000 = 16$

The general formula for the performance improvement factor associated with contexts is given by:

- factor = $c^{(s-1)}$

The same example with past, present, and future contexts i.e., 3 contexts would give a performance factor improvement of:

- factor = $3^{(5-1)} = 81$

From these considerations, we can see that as well as satisfying a functional requirement, contexts have the potential to yield substantial system performance benefits.

A supplementary approach is to categorise nodes. Node inputs and outputs can only occur in certain configurations.

For node inputs, we can have either no inputs, an *is* input only, a *has* input only, or an *is* and a *has* input; no other combinations are possible. So, we have four categories only, and we can group nodes into each of these. This means that when we are searching for a node corresponding to *lady* say, as in the previous example, we can determine which category the node belongs to in the sentence subnet, and then confine any search to the appropriate one(s) out of the four categories. So, for example, if a node in the sentence subnet has an *is* input and a *has* input, then we need only search this category. If a node has an *is* input only, then we need to search two categories, the one with an *is* input only and the one with an *is* and a *has* input.

This particular strategy gives the potential to reduce the nodes searched by a factor of about two. But the performance increase with the previous example would be about:

- performance improvement = 2^5 = 32

Combined with the improvement due to contexts we could see a typical performance improvement of:

- performance improvement = 81 x 32 = 2,592

To summarise therefore, there appear to be a number of strategies which can capitalise on the characteristics of the structure of the mental model to achieve significant reductions in the time taken to search the main net for subnets associated with input sentences.

Mind and brain operation

It is interesting to speculate whether the mind and brain engage in similar processes to the one outlined in the previous section, to locate subnets within a mental model main net.

We have suggested in the section how one might approach the problem of subnet location using a serial processor, and the timing challenges that this poses.

The individual neuro-synaptic elements within the brain are known to be very very slow compared with contemporary processor hardware. But we suggest that the nature of this particular problem, involving as it does, the graphical structure of the main net and subnet, would lend itself to a parallel neuro-synaptic wired approach. We suggest that this is something at which the brain would excel, yielding acceptably fast search times even with the comparatively slow brain logic.

Philosophical aspects of mental models

At this point, just prior to the conclusion of this part of the book, we pause to take a brief detour, to look at one or two of the philosophical implications of mental models.

The Aristotelian, versus the *is-has,* sentence

The Aristotelian sentence is generally represented by an assertion having a value of true or false e.g., *all men are mortal.* Aristotelian logic is based on manipulation of the true or false values of a succession of such sentences (Cryan, Shatil, & Mayblin, The Syllogism, 2013) e.g.

- *all men are mortal*
- *Socrates is a man*
- *Socrates is mortal*

But let's go back a step or two to see to what degree Aristotelian logic considerations affect our everyday mundane communications with each other in the real world. We begin by suggesting that statistically 90 or perhaps even 99 per cent of all human communications, often in the form of sentences, must be truthful and valid, either absolutely or in the sincere belief of their authors.

To see why, let's just think, if a significant proportion of human communications could not be relied upon as being truthful and valid, then we suggest that human society and the human economic machine would not work very efficiently, or even not work at all.

This doesn't mean there are not plenty of untruths around, particularly in the political, criminal, and emotional spheres.

Nevertheless, taken as a purely statistical proportion of all communications we suggest these are small. We generally find the price we pay for something is the price marked on it, not some other arbitrary figure. The weather forecast may be wrong, but the forecaster will not generally just invent some arbitrary figure for the temperature; it will be based on measurement and calculation. If your spouse says they will pick the kids up from school, then this is generally what we expect will happen; your spouse will not deliberately lie. In fact, we generally expect the whole gamut of routine, mundane, humdrum, everyday communications to be generally truthful and valid. To repeat, for human society and the human economic machine to work, this has to be so.

Looking at things from a Darwinian point of view, if there was competition between efficient and inefficient human groups, the efficient groups would tend win out. According to evolutionary principles there would be natural selection in favour of efficient groups i.e., there would be natural selection in favour of groups engaging in truthful and valid communications.

We suggest that all this implies that the amount of information carried by the true or false value of the average sentence is not high. If we don't have an explicit value for it, for a particular mundane sentence we encounter during the day, but guess that it is true and valid, then we are going to be right 90 to 99 per cent of the time. So, if we accept that the truth value is not carrying much information in the average sentence, then where does the bulk of sentence information reside?

The *is-has* mental model sentence is generally represented as a mental model update not unlike a database update, where the mental model is regarded as a sort of database. In this, at least one component of the average sentence represents a location on the mental model, and at least one component represents data to be added to the mental model at that location, to update it. So, if we have the sentence

• *the dark red balloon has a long string with a knot*

In this, the phrase *the dark red balloon* gives us the location on the mental model, the phrase *a long string with a knot* gives us most of the data to be added at this location, and the verb *has* gives the remainder, indicating that the new data is to be linked in using the relation *has*. The exact mechanism was discussed in detail in the earlier section *Updating our mental model*. We noted earlier that some sentences may update more than one location with more than one data item.

So, in conclusion, we suggest that this is where most of sentence's information resides, in the mental model location data and in the model update data. Being heretical perhaps, we suggest the true or false value for the average everyday mundane sentence is almost irrelevant.

Set theory implications

Is there a relationship between mathematical set theory and *is-has* expressions? There are a number of definitions of a mathematical set; here is Cantor's definition (Cantor, 1895).

• *A set is a gathering together into a whole of definite distinct objects of our perception or of our thought – which are called elements of a set.*

However, if we have a simple sentence such as *A has B*, then we suggest that this sentence implies both that *A* is something that is capable of *having* something and that *B* is something that is capable of being *had* by something, in this case *A*. In other words, we are implicitly defining *A* to be a set and *B* to be a set member, and rather more specifically that the defined set *A* has the defined set member *B*.

With a similar sentence using *is* such as *X is Y*, one could mount a similar argument that *X* is being asserted to a member of set *Y*. Note in contrast with the *has* example, the positions of references to the set member *X* and the set *Y* have exchanged. However, as discussed in the earlier *Part I* section *To be*, we prefer in this text to view *is* expressions as relating things that we can directly measure or perceive with our senses, and reserve *has* expressions to describe set membership relationships.

Based on these arguments, should we perhaps be using *is-has* relationships as a basis for mathematics, rather than set theory? We suggest that we can actually describe set theory using *is-has* sentences. But is the reverse true, can we describe *is-has* sentences using set theory? We leave you to judge.

Forgiving nature of semantic processes

We have no way of knowing if everyone forms the same mental model of the real world. Indeed, we do not know if human mental models bear any relationship whatsoever to the semantic network based mental models we have been discussing. Another factor is that even with the latter, there may be some argument and controversy surrounding the methodology described; there may be variant methods which would more truly represent the linguistic semantics involved.

However, there is a compensating factor contributing to the utility of the mental models so far described. Suppose that the mental model and corresponding main net graph we generate for *Jack is climbing up the hill* is less than truly representative of the semantics. Suppose we subsequently process the query *who is climbing up the hill?* As long as we use exactly the same methodology to build the subnet for this query as we did for the original model, then the query subnet will bear a strong relationship to the corresponding *Jack* subnet within the main net. When we execute the query and carry out an isomorphic search of the main net, there is a good chance we will still find some correspondence.

So, as long as we are entirely consistent with our use of the methodology, even if this methodology contains misconceptions, there is a strong chance that in practical use, errors will tend to cancel. Maybe, dare we suggest it, this is what happens with human mental models. Maybe we each form our models in a different way. But as long as we remain consistent in processing queries on our own model, differences will tend to cancel out, and we will still have a working system.

Conclusion

At this point, we've reached the end of *Part II, Dialogues & Mental Models*. Hopefully, you've found it interesting, informative, and thought-provoking.

We are going to move shortly in *Part IV* onto a discussion of the *AI Dialog* software demonstrator. *AI Dialog* gives a practical demonstration of much, but not all of the theory described in *Part I* and *Part II. AI Dialog* is able to engage in a conversation with the user, accepting plain English input in the form of either text or speech, or a mixture, and responding in the same. *AI Dialog* comprehends user input and builds an internal mental model from this, of the type we've been discussing. It subsequently uses the model to respond to user queries testing this comprehension. *Appendix A*, which follows *Part IV* describes its operation and characteristics in detail, and lists sites from where a free download may be obtained.

The theory in *Part II* is supported by a *YouTube®* lecture of about one hour duration entitled *Artificial General Intelligence, A New Approach, Part II Dialogues and Mental Models*.

PART III

SIGNIFICANT ISSUES

No web connect, neural network or training

The *AI Dialog* demonstrator software described next, is based on the theory of *Part I* and *Part II* and does not require, and indeed does not support, any connection to the web. From *Part I* and *Part II*, you will note that *AI Dialog* does not need to make use of neural network technology. As a consequence of this approach, we think you will agree that a technology based on the principles described here has no stochastic elements, and that its operation is entirely deterministic and transparent. You may also have observed that the concept of training *AI Dialog* to recognise language constructs is not a requirement either.

Potential for self-description

It must be obvious that this discourse which describes the *is-has* theory and how a mental model may be based on it, is itself composed of English sentences. But the theory, if you remember, says that all English sentences can be analysed in terms of *is-has* expressions, which can subsequently be incorporated into a mental model. So, an intriguing question which arises, is whether we can use the theory to incorporate into the mental model a description of the principles behind that very same model. The key question we are asking is, can the technology describe itself? If this is possible, then where does this lead exactly? This is an exciting notion that is certainly open to future research.

Popular concerns regarding super intelligence

There are very understandable popular concerns about the evolution of AGI. These are reflected in a fear that AGI development might result in a system which could autonomously and uncontrollably evolve itself into a super intelligence, with a capability far beyond that of a human being's. Would such a super intelligence be one which would perhaps not be driven by any human values and would perhaps not have humanity's best interests at heart? Alternatively, would such a super intelligence be one which would perhaps simply make humanity obsolete, as there would be nothing at all that a human being could do which the machine could not do much more flawlessly and much faster.

To address these concerns various public governmental and private bodies are in the course of being set up, to attempt to limit and control AGI development, to try to forestall any of the eventualities mentioned and protect humanity from the possibility of harm. However, human international and commercial competition being what it is, you may find yourself sceptical about the likely effectiveness of any legislation resulting from proposals by these bodies.

The following section attempts to supply some possible hints of comfort or reassurance, but which, to be perfectly frank, may or may not be valid. Nevertheless, we believe these things are worth saying, as they have not, as far as we are aware, have been said before.

The principle of natural limitations

Think about a simple bridge consisting of a beam supported on pillars at either end. If we extend the span of the bridge by moving the end pillars further apart, the beam will eventually start to sag in the middle due to its own weight. This will limit the length of the single unsupported span bridge. We might try to overcome the problem by increasing the thickness of the beam, but this will increase its weight and it will still eventually sag in the middle at some point. Nature, the structure of the Universe, call it what you will, has imposed its own natural limitations on what is feasible from an engineering point of view. We are prevented from building a single unsupported single span bridge of more than a certain length.

Einstein discovered that the faster an object moves, the more massive it becomes. When we try to accelerate a particle in a particle accelerator, the faster we get the particle to move, the more massive it becomes, and the more power we need to make it move even faster. At close to the speed of light, the power needed becomes so great, we cannot supply it. Starships may regularly exceed the speed of light in Star Trek but with practical engineering at present we cannot make them do it. Nature has again imposed its own natural limitations on what is feasible.

We can make a computer chip perform calculations twice as fast by doubling its clock frequency, but the penalty nature imposes in the form of increased power consumption is not proportional to the clock frequency but to the square of this frequency. So, the power consumption is not twice as much but four times. In an extreme case, if we increased the calculation rate by a factor of ten, say, nature would demand one hundred times as much power. Nature again is beginning to impose limitations on what is feasible.

A few years ago, we started to encounter similar limitations in the development AGI software. A fundamental need which arose was so search a large complex pattern for the presence of a small sub-pattern within it. This was described earlier in the section *Isomorphic subgraph search*. As a child you might have come across a puzzle, where an artist had drawn a picture, of a garden say, and hidden within the picture drawings of garden implements such as a spade, rake, or trowel, which you were challenged to find. Our problem is of a similar kind.

It is a problem which appears in different guises in many scientific fields, for example analysing complex molecular structures in chemistry, but it also appears to be a fundamental requirement in the implementation of AGI. In our case the large pattern consists of so-called nodes or vertices connected by edges. The sub-pattern consists of a much smaller number of nodes connected by edges. Computer software of course is involved in searching for the sub-pattern, and it is a fundamental requirement to calculate how long a computer program might take to run with given sizes of containing pattern and sub-pattern.

Interestingly, as described in the earlier section *Subgraph search time*, this computation time turns out not to be directly proportional to the sizes of the patterns involved but to exponential powers of their sizes. In practice, this yields some eye-watering numbers even for very modestly sized patterns. For example, with just a hundred nodes in the pattern and four nodes in the sub-pattern, in a worst case, we are looking at an order of 100 million program cycles. But one hundred nodes is absolutely nothing compared with the requirement for even slightly intelligent computer software, which in practice needs orders upon orders of larger values for the numbers of nodes.

We suggest therefore, that the computational resources needed to solve such a problem within a realistic timescale, i.e., before the user dies of old age, even with the spectacularly high speeds of modern processors, are possibly going to eventually exceed what it is practicable to provide. Some of the numbers involved in computations like this could well exceed the estimated number of stars in the firmament or even the number of their component atoms. We therefore suggest that it just very, very faintly possible, and we can really put it no more strongly than that, that Nature will again impose restrictions on what is feasible in terms of the development of super intelligence from AGI. But then again, maybe Nature will not impose such restrictions; it's only our guess or perhaps even hope, based admittedly on very, very slender evidence indeed.

In the world of Wonder Woman, Superman or Mr Spock, a character's flick of the wrist or a moment or two's thought, sorts out incredibly challenging physical or mental problems. But in the real-world, Nature is a very stern arbiter indeed of what is feasible in terms of real human engineering, and more often than not says: thus far but no farther. You may be familiar with the saying *Man proposes but God disposes* (Kempis, 2023). In the real-world of human engineering, man or woman may well try the proposing, but God (or Nature if you will) really will do the disposing.

Finally, it is interesting to speculate whether evolution has already trodden the super intelligence development path, thoroughly explored it, and decided exactly what the optimum solution is, given Nature's apparent underlying restrictions. Could is just be, therefore, that real, truly creative intelligence, as super as it is ever going to get, is already with us, in the form of that few pounds of grey matter residing between our ears?

Complex systems from elemental parts

If you have been convinced by the *is-has* theory that all English sentences can be resolved entirely into just a series of elemental *is-has* expressions, then you may feel some sense of depression. Are we saying that every sentence in the plays of Shakespeare, the poetry of Milton, the Bible, the novels of Austen and Bronte can be reduced to just a series of *is-has* expressions? Well, if you believe the theory, the simple answer has to be, yes. Does this diminish the significance of these monumental works in any way? We would suggest the answer is, certainly not. The fact that complex systems turn out to be built from very simple elemental components does not diminish their wonder in any way. Starting from basics, the English alphabet is only 26 letters, and yet every word in these works is constructed from it, and in turn every sentence from these words. But we also encounter many other complex systems constructed from even more elemental components. The following section gives just one example.

The digital computer and the nand gate

In theory at least, we can construct most of a digital computer, characterised by the internals of a mobile phone, laptop or tablet from just one type of elemental component, the nand gate, or its close relative, the nor gate. The following diagram gives you a flavour. The topmost figure shows the basic nand gate together with the truth table relating its inputs and outputs. If both inputs A and B have any combination of logical values except both true, then the output of the gate Q is true, otherwise it is false.

The second figure shows that we can interconnect two nand gates to give a latch or memory element. This circuit is capable of storing or remembering a single binary digit or bit. If the set signal S is made true with the reset R false, the output Q goes true and the inverted output Q' goes false, and this state is remembered whilst S and R both revert to true. Similarly, if the reset R is made true with the set S false, the output Q goes false and the inverted output Q' goes true and this state is remembered again whilst S and R both revert to true. Eight of these memory elements, side by side, are capable of storing a byte of data. Eight million of these are capable of storing a Mbyte of data.

The third figure shows an adder, capable of adding together two binary digits or bits A and B. The circuit also generates a carry out Co. We can chain a number of these circuits together to enable two numbers each represented by an arbitrary number of bits, 32 say, to give a circuit capable of adding these two numbers together. We chain stages together by connecting the carry in Ci of one stage to the carry out Co of the previous (less significant) stage. The carry in Ci of the least significant stage is held at the value false.

In a similar way by adding a so-called shift register we can build circuits to do multiplication and division, and any other logical or arithmetic operation we choose.

There is not quite enough logic here to build the whole of a computer processor and memory system, we need what are termed clock circuits. These are used for two purposes, The first is to overcome a physical problem of large gate complexes in that they need a settling time before they produce valid logical outputs from a set of logical inputs. The second is that complex computation has a need to feed back precisely timed intermediate logical and arithmetic results into earlier logic stages. Interesting, the brain also seems to use clock circuits too, termed the alpha, beta, delta and theta rhythms plus others, perhaps for the same reasons.

The other absentees from our logic circuits are those specialised devices which provide the audible, visual, and tactile human-computer interfaces, and those which provide radio communications to remote equipments.

Nevertheless, it is theoretically possible to build 90% or more of a computer system from just large numbers of the humble nand or nor gate. In practice, for engineering reasons a range of other gate types are used in computer processors and memories. A typical computer processor chip or Gbyte of memory contains billions of gates.

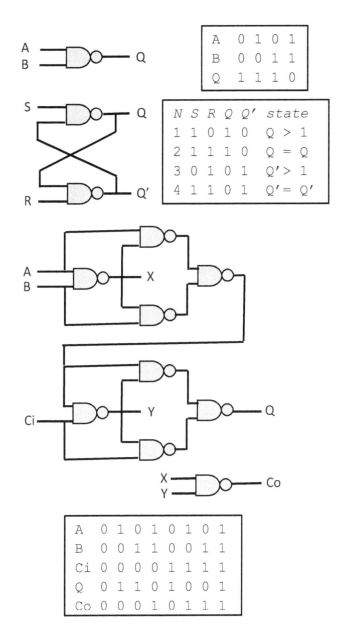

A	0	1	0	1
B	0	0	1	1
Q	1	1	1	0

N	S	R	Q	Q′	state
1	1	0	1	0	Q > 1
2	1	1	1	0	Q = Q
3	0	1	0	1	Q′> 1
4	1	1	0	1	Q′= Q′

A	0	1	0	1	0	1	0	1
B	0	0	1	1	0	0	1	1
Ci	0	0	0	0	1	1	1	1
Q	0	1	1	0	1	0	0	1
Co	0	0	0	1	0	1	1	1

A final word

Whether an English semantic analysis based solely on *is-has* relationships, as described in this book, represents a valid philosophical approach to this task, only time will tell. But the *is-has* mental model that can be built from this type of analysis, does shows promise as an avenue to conversational AI software, possibly moving marginally, dare we say it, in the direction of intelligent thought. No insuperable problems have been encountered in the research, so far, with the *AI Dialog* decoding of English language discourses and the building of mental models from them, or, in response to plain English queries, locating model data and synthesising plain English replies.

We have seen that some of these replies may also involve a significant degree of logical reasoning to synthesise the result – the logic does tend to be subsumed into pattern recognition – but is present, nevertheless. One can envisage increasing the complexity and sophistication of the English language and concepts understandable by the demonstrator, with, at present, no especial obstruction to development, other than the length of time and degree of effort involved.

Finally, does the method of analysing English based solely on *is-has* relationships, and the building of a mental model using these, shed any light on the way the human mind and brain might process and understand language? Are *is* and *has* concepts fundamental to our way of thinking, or not? We put forward some views on this topic in the earlier *Part I* section *The origins of human language*. Do the mind and brain do it in a similar way, or do they carry out the process in a completely different manner? If the mind and brain are confined to *is-has* concepts alone, then as mentioned earlier, it may actually be impossible for us to think about, or to construct any sentence which is not based on these concepts. We can only speculate on these matters.

PART IV

THE AI DIALOG DEMONSTRATOR

Introduction

The *AI Dialog* software demonstrator is based wholly on the theory laid out in *Part I* and *Part II* of this book. The demonstrator is able to engage with the user in a spoken or textual dialogue composed of plain English sentences. The demonstrator analyses spoken or textual input sentences and reduces them entirely to *is-has* expressions as covered by the theory of *Part I*. The demonstrator then uses these to establish or augment an internal mental model, based on *is-has* semantic networks as covered by the theory of *Part II*. Subsequently, in response to plain English queries, testing comprehension or requiring logic or calculation, the demonstrator determines answers by examining its mental model and, where necessary, performing the required logic or calculation, based mostly on the isomorphic search principles. It then synthesises plain English sentences in reply to these queries, as covered also by the theory of *Part II*.

The *AI Dialog* software is publicly available via a download, details of which are given in the following *Appendix A*. It runs on a PC or tablet under *Windows 10®* onwards and requires about 1 Mbyte of memory.

Objectives

The *AI Dialog* software is not a commercial end product, but rather it has been designed to satisfy the following research objectives. These objectives are generally associated with experiments to prove (or disprove) the hypotheses of *Part I* and *Part II*.

Firstly, can arbitrary real-world sentences really be broken down into *is-has* relationships? Coupled with this, is it a practical proposition to design software to perform the syntactic and semantic analysis of sentences necessary to extract these component relationships?

Secondly, is it feasible to build in computer memory, and subsequently augment, a mental model based on the *is-has* relationships extracted from sentences, using *is-has* semantic networks? Coupled with this, is it practical proposition to design graph-based computer memory data structures capable of efficiently representing these networks?

Thirdly, can we really implement comprehension queries and carry out logic and, if not higher mathematics, at least simple arithmetic calculations, using the semantic network-based mental model? Coupled with this, can we use software to carry out efficient isomorphic subgraph searches on the mental model graph, which would appear to be necessitated by the previous?

Fourthly, is it feasible to use software to perform sentence synthesis to build replies to comprehension, logic, and arithmetic queries from a graph-based *is-has* semantic network representing a mental model?

Generally, can all the above-described procedures be

implemented using both speech and textual input sentences or indeed a mixture of both.

We can see that these research objectives taken together are trying to provide a definitive answer to the fundamental question of: can *is-has* sentence analysis, coupled with the building of *is-has* semantic networks representing mental models, really provide an avenue into general or strong AI?

Limitations

There are some substantial limitations to the present version of the *AI Dialog* software demonstrator. However, new developments show promise that these limitations need not always be present.

Firstly, the demonstrator needs to use a formal grammar along the lines of Fowler (Fowler & Fowler, 1989) but substantially simplified and reduced. However, in practice this grammar is fairly sophisticated, allowing, for example, unlimited nesting of quite complex clauses. Nevertheless, sentences are constrained to follow formal grammar rules, and input sentences not following these rules cannot be handled and are reported as erroneous by the logic.

Secondly, spoken rather than textual input is problematic. The speech recognition software often gets spoken sentences wrong. To surmount these problems a range of word and phrase level sentence verbal editing tools have been provided. Nevertheless, speech input is at times less than satisfactory and far more cumbersome than it might be. Textual input, which is available also, steps around these problems but its use is in a way is an admission of failure to achieve one of the fundamental objectives of a spoken dialogue.

Thirdly, the isomorphic search algorithms are slow and

unsophisticated and with slower processors result in sluggish sentence processing. This is particularly so with functions such as the multi-sentence synthesis associated with requests to the demonstrator to generate a description of something.

Fourthly, substantial parts of the theory described in Part I and Part II are not implemented in the publicly available download version. These include quantifiers, the passive voice, contexts, meanings, and use of anchors during sentence synthesis to give sentence stresses. The demonstrator provides only very basic support for indirect objects. The absence of contexts means that in the download version verb tense flagging is handled temporarily differently, as mentioned following.

Remarks on input treatment

Verb tense flagging

In the download version, verb tense flagging is achieved by adding a reference to each relationship edge, named past, present or future. Further tenses could be added, for example future conditional. There could be past, present and future forms of inverted verbs reflected in *was ... by, is ... by* and *will be ... by*, and associated with the passive voice, but the demonstrator at present does not implement them.

Nouns

Nouns are represented just as instances, as discussed under the *Part II* section *The influence of determiners*. Any word is recognised as a noun if it appears in the appropriate position for a noun, and not recognised as another part of speech, for example, a determiner. If the noun instance is absent from the main net, considering any qualifiers, then a new noun instance is added. Otherwise, an existing instance is referenced.

Adjective/adverb strings

A problem with adjective/adverb strings preceding nouns is associated with lack of world knowledge. In the phrase *The very large, dark red balloon ...* we know, from world knowledge, that *very* is an adverb qualifying *large* and that *large* qualifies *balloon* and not the following *dark*, and that *dark* could be regarded as a sort of adverb qualifying *red*, which in turn qualifies *balloon*. The present version of the demonstrator does not distinguish between adjectives and adverbs and treats both on more or less the same basis. The problem of association is avoided in the demonstrator by requiring the use of the commas shown in the example. Any adjective/adverb not followed by a comma qualifies the next adjective, but otherwise qualifies the noun. An alternative approach which would help in some cases, but not all, would be to differentiate adjectives and adverbs, or adjectives used in an adverbial sense.

On phrase or sentence regeneration from a subnet, the same adjective/adverb ordering associated with the original input is potentially recoverable, provided that ordering data is retained by the demonstrator, but this is not the case at present.

Definitions

The demonstrator at present does not build a subnet from a definition, but holds it as one or more sentences invoked as required. The demonstrator also does not support *meanings* as described in *Part II* section *Meanings*.

Sharing

As mentioned in *Part I* a variant of possession uses the verb *sharing*. If we have *Jack and Jill each shares the pail*, this is represented as in the following figure. The demonstrator treats as erroneous expressions such as *Jack and Jill each has the pail*, where there is only one *pail*.

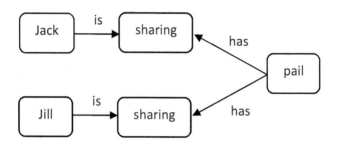

Principles of operation

The diagram following outlines the principles of operation of the AI Dialog demonstrator.

Input Output Interface

This provides a speech and textual interface to the user. The user may speak or type, and if necessary edit, sentences, and definitions and then input them to the demonstrator and see results from these. This also provides an interface to the file system so that sentences, definitions, and results may be written to or read from the file system. Included within this also are interactive Help and Tuition facilities. Included also are facilities to monitor the content of the semantic network mental model graph; any input definitions; and graph traversal (subvocalisation) during sentence synthesis.

Lexical Processing

This is concerned with recognising and marking particular word types within a sentence. It is also concerned with conversion of verbs to participles, conversion of plurals to singulars, recognition of definite and indefinite determiners, recognition of clause separators and recognition of prepositions, amongst other word types. Essentially each sentence is rationalised and prepared for syntax analysis. As shown in the diagram, errors may be reported during processing, and these are reported back to the Input Output Interface.

Syntax Analyser

This analyses a sentence on more or less formal lines, using top-down analysis, firstly breaking the sentence into subject and object/complement clause groups, separated by the sentence main verb. Each clause group is then analysed into main and subsidiary clauses. Each clause is then broken down into sets of *is-has* expressions. One set is associated with the subject and another set is associated with the object/complement. Associated with each set is an anchor node, determined during the analysis. Associated with each set is also a definite or indefinite determiner. If the indefinite determiner happens to be a cardinal, then special note is taken of this as it will often result in an effective multiplication of the *is-has* sets associated with it. The main verb is held separately. This whole dataset is then handed over to the Semantics Analyser. Again, as shown in the diagram, any errors are reported back to the Input Output Interface.

Semantics Analyser

A key component of the Semantics Analyser is the isomorphic search mechanism. The subject and object/complement *is-has* sets are effectively subject and object/complement subnets. The analyser uses each of these in separate isomorphic searches. The number of results each of these returns is used in logic associated with the definite or indefinite articles to validity check sentence semantics. This type of check for erroneous semantics was covered in the *Part II* section *The influence of determiners*. As shown in the diagram, the analyser has a connection to the Input Output Interface both for the reporting of semantic errors and returning the results of queries.

Main Net Graph

The Main Net Graph is based on a directed graph data structure as described under the *Part II* section *Data structure of the mental model*. The main net accumulates data as sentences are input.

Sentence Synthesiser

The sentence synthesiser is used to respond to requests such as *describe Jack*. In this example, the node *Jack* is located as part of a trivial isomorphic search. This node is then used as a starting point for a graph traversal. Each part of the tree stemming from this results in a word or clause synthesis as described in the *Part II* section *Sentence synthesis*. Internally, the traversal algorithm makes use of the *View* mechanism described in the *Part II* section *Viewing just parts of the mental model*.

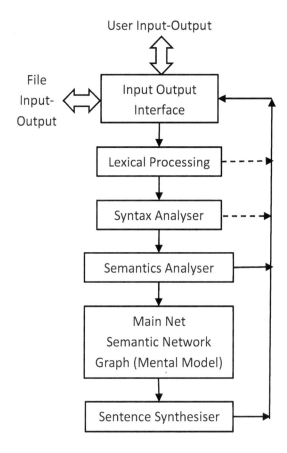

Future development paths

The development of the demonstrator to date opens up many new potential paths of enquiry. The following are just a few.

Transient memory

We are used to devoting our attention and thoughts to a

particular problem, and then once we have achieved a solution, remembering that solution only, and dismissing the steps involved in arriving at it. This is not unlike a storage allocation and deallocation activity which often occurs whilst contemporary computer software is running. We could handle it with a *temporary* context as follows:

- *thinking about Tom* (all further storage is in a *temporary* context flagged as *about Tom*)
- *Tom is a doctor* (the context is used and results in consulting of the *doctor* definition)
- *Tom is caring and compassionate.* (further context storage is used for the *doctor* definition)
- *Tom has a medical degree.* (even more context storage is used for the *doctor* definition)
- further sentences then form some conclusion based on the previous
- *forgetting about Tom.* (all *temporary* context storage used since *thinking about Tom is* released for re-use)

The existing rollback facility of the demonstrator goes a little way, but not very far, along this path.

Subvocalisation

We saw with the example *Jack says 'Jill will carry the pail'* that we can retain a sentence such as *Jill will carry the pail* in an undecoded form, to be decoded later if we wish. We have also seen that we can synthesise a sentence from a subnet constituting part of the mental model. At present such a sentence is presented to the user as a query reply. But we could synthesise sentences and retain them in internal memory. This leads to the possibility of a rich internal interchange of sentences being synthesised from the mental model and later re-analysed to add back into the model, as the demonstrator thinks about things. We suggest that this is a feature of our own thought processes; we constantly seem to subvocalise, forming phrases or sentences or entire dialogues in our minds as we reflect upon things.

English as the programming language

Students learning a foreign language generally begin by being taught the elements of the target language in their own language. But once they have achieved some competence, more advanced tuition takes place in the target language itself. We pose the question therefore whether it might become feasible to continue programming of the *AI Dialog* demonstrator in English itself, once the demonstrator is able to understand a basic useful subset. That subset would tend to refer to the demonstrator's internal features and mechanisms and have a basic vocabulary related to these.

Fragmentary non-formal input

As mentioned earlier, at present demonstrator input is constrained by formal grammatical rules. In the long run, it seems feasible to allow a much more informal input in parallel with the formal one. This might be based on the demonstrator trying to guess what the user is trying to say and fitting it into one of the formal structures, possibly with some user interaction along the lines of *is this what you are trying to say* ... There is some tenuous evidence, obtained from work with the present demonstrator, that syntactic and semantic sentence analysis based on abandoning the formal grammar processing might actually be more straightforward to implement. One might half expect this, as one presumes Nature would not deliberately make it difficult for our minds and brains to decode and encode our speech. In hearing or reading a sentence, do we really decode it into the formal grammar constructs, or do we take a more direct path to the *is-has* expressions that we theorise a sentence is composed of?

(This page is intentionally blank)

APPENDIX A

THE AI DIALOG DEMONSTRATOR

The *AI Dialog* software demonstrator runs on a PC, laptop or tablet using *Windows 10®* and requires about 1 Mbyte of storage. It may be downloaded for free using any of the three methods below.

http://dx.doi.org/10.17632/zhv2wfnprv

Type the above reference (which is a Digital Object Identifier or DOI) into your browser and click *Search*. This will take you to a research data repository page with instructions on how to download and install the demonstrator application.

http://doi.org/10.5281/zenodo.8298365

Type the above reference (another DOI) into your browser and click *Search*. This will take you to another research data repository page with instructions on how to download and install the demonstrator application.

http://doi.org/10.6084/m9.figshare.23613804

Type the above reference (another DOI) into your browser and click *Search*. This will take you to another research data repository page with instructions on how to download and install the demonstrator application.

When the application has been downloaded, installed, and started, follow the pop-up message instructions, which lead to an interactive tutorial module, giving instructions on how to use the demonstrator.

The download file has a *Documentation* folder containing two PDF files: *Appendix I – Tutorial Lessons, and Appendix II – AI Dialog Specification.* There is no need to consult either initially as the demonstrator contains a quick start tutorial module. The demonstrator will accept U.K. or U.S. spelling during conversations.

The following description applies to *AI Dialog Software Version 4.1 Alpha.*

An actual run of the demonstrator appears in a *YouTube*® video of about twenty minutes duration, entitled *Artificial General Intelligence, A New Approach, AI Dialog Demonstration.*

When the demonstrator starts, by default, it is in speech mode. In this mode, it expects speech input from the microphone and responds with speech output to the headphones or speakers.

When the demonstrator starts in speech mode it shows the initial screen of Figure A - 1.

Along the bottom of this screen are two pushbuttons labelled *Text IO* and *Exit.* If *Text IO* is clicked, the demonstrator switches to text mode. In this mode, it expects text input from the keyboard and responds with text output to the screen.

When text mode is selected, the demonstrator switches to

show the screen of Figure A - 2. This screen is the same as Figure A - 1, except that the *Text IO* pushbutton changes to *Speech IO*, the *Exit* pushbutton remains the same and additional pushbuttons *Enter/Got It, Clear, Rollback, New - Reset, Open, Delete* and *Tutorial* appear. If the *Speech IO* pushbutton is clicked, the demonstrator reverts to speech mode again and displays the screen of Figure A - 1.

The function of the other pushbuttons in each mode will be described in the following sections. In speech mode or text mode, many demonstrator functions are common. The following sections indicate where functions are differentiated depending on mode.

Figure A - 1

Figure A - 2

Initial Screen Layout

Via the lower left window within the initial screen, in either case, shown in greater detail later, plain English sentences appear for input to the demonstrator, which later indicates if it has understood them or not. These sentences are either spoken in speech mode, or typed in text mode. Sentences either provide new data, or are used to test the demonstrator's comprehension of existing data, or carry out reasoning on it.

The demonstrator builds an internal mental model from each data sentence, augmenting the model as each sentence is input. Each sentence testing the demonstrator's comprehension or logic results in it consulting the model, determining the answer required, and formatting this as a plain English sentence reply. This reply is spoken in speech mode, but is displayed as text in either mode.

The upper left window within the screen, shown in greater detail later, logs the conversation as text, showing each user sentence and each demonstrator response to that sentence.

In a right-hand tab window, shown in greater detail later, the internal mental model may be viewed at any time, and shows any data being added to the model, derived from the latest input sentence.

A plain English *definition* sentence, described fully later, may define the meaning of something to the demonstrator. A further right-hand tab window, shown in greater detail later, enables any definitions input so far and remembered by the demonstrator, to be viewed. Again, these definitions are input via the spoken word in speech mode or typed in text mode.

Finally, for complex comprehension testing using an input

describe sentence command, a further right-hand tab window, shown in greater detail later, displays the demonstrator's internal logical processes, as the multi-sentence plain English description is built up.

In either mode, the demonstrator incorporates tutorial facilities which show the user the rules governing the structures of typical plain English sentences that may be input. Using these facilities, example sentences may recalled from a file and input successively to the demonstrator by the user, to show the user the demonstrator's capabilities, illustrating any additions to the mental model resulting from data sentences, or the demonstrator's plain English replies to comprehension or logic testing sentences.

The demonstrator also has a facility to enable user sentence input to be recorded in a text file, which may be recalled at a later date, to cause the demonstrator to rebuild the mental model associated with it. The demonstrator supports multiple files of this type.

Screen detail

Figure A - 3 shows the left-hand of the screen in greater detail. The top banner shows the software version e.g., *AI Dialog Software Version 4.1 Alpha*. In either mode, the menu bar contains:

- *Bugs* – if clicked, this shows a message box with text about any demonstrator bugs
- *About* – if clicked, this shows a message box with text about the demonstrator copyright
- *Contact* – if clicked, this shows a message box with text about developer contact details

A panel is headed *DIALOG INTERFACE* and contains text boxes.

The lower text box headed *Sentence to Input* is where each sentence for input to the demonstrator is recorded. This sentence results from either spoken or typed input, depending on mode. The box also displays any error information. In speech mode, this error information is also spoken by the demonstrator.

The upper text box headed, in the figure, *~AI Dialog/Dialog Files/default* is where a log of the conversation with the demonstrator is recorded showing each sentence the user inputs and the demonstrator's response to that sentence. The box heading shown is representative of text mode, where the file path name of a file where the conversation is being recorded is shown. In speech mode this contracts to just the root file name i.e., *default*. This heading changes during tutorials to show the name of the lesson being executed.

Text mode pushbuttons

In text mode, various pushbuttons appear at the foot of the screen, but are invisible in speech mode. Their use in text mode is as follows:

- *Enter/Got It* – to cause a typed sentence to be submitted to the demonstrator (*Enter*), or to acknowledge an error or other response (*Got It*)
- *Clear/Previous* – to either clear the sentence input box or recall an earlier sentence

Figure A - 4 shows additional pushbuttons to the right of the above:

- *Rollback* – to rollback the previous sentence and remove its memory from the mental model; this can be used repeatedly if required
- *New - Reset* – to open a new text file in which a new conversation can be recorded, or to reset or empty an existing text file and delete any associated mental model, but retain the file ready to record new input.
- *Open* – to open an existing text file and recall a conversation from it, together with its associated mental model
- *Delete* – to delete an existing text file and any associated mental model.

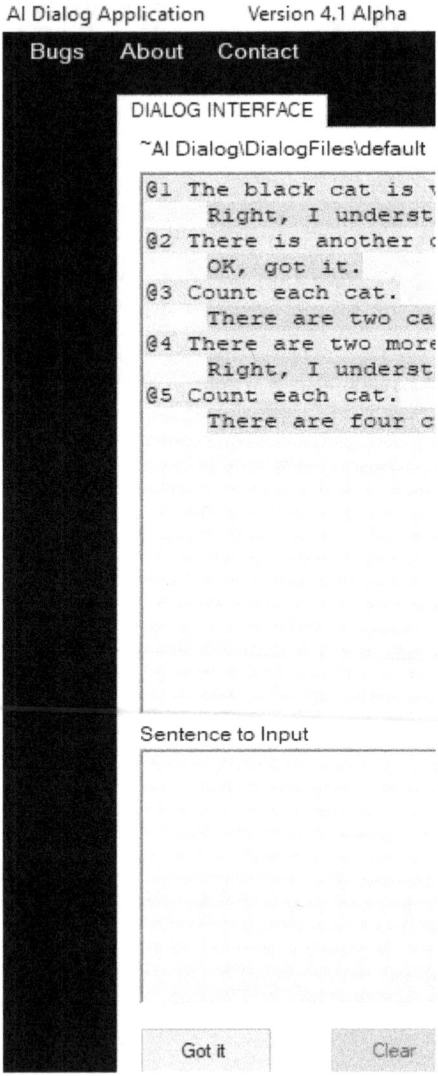

AI Dialog Application   Version 4.1 Alpha

Bugs   About   Contact

DIALOG INTERFACE

~AI Dialog\DialogFiles\default

@1 The black cat is ʋ
      Right, I underst
@2 There is another ᴄ
      OK, got it.
@3 Count each cat.
      There are two ca
@4 There are two more
      Right, I underst
@5 Count each cat.
      There are four c

Sentence to Input

Got it   Clear

Figure A - 3

210

Figure A - 4

Figure A - 5 shows the right-hand side of the screen in greater detail.

Selection of the *Mental Model* tab causes the text box below to show the contents of the demonstrator's mental model.

Selection of the *Definitions* tab causes the text box below to show any definitions that the demonstrator is remembering.

Selection of the *Subvocalisation* tab causes the text box below to show the demonstrator's logic processes during its multi-sentence response to a *describe* request.

The pushbuttons at the foot of the screen, with the exception of *Speech IO/Text IO*, again only appear in text mode, when they are used as follows:

> • *Delete* – described previously
> • *Tutorial/Quit Tutorial* – to invoke (*Tutorial*) or quit (*Quit Tutorial*) the tutorial facility
> • *Speech IO/Text IO* – to switch to speech mode (*Speech IO*) or switch back to text mode (*Text IO*)

Figure A - 5

Figure A - 6 shows a further pushbutton to the far right:

> • *Exit* – to exit the demonstrator; the current
> conversation is automatically preserved in a text file.

Exit

Figure A - 6

Speech mode

Tutorial facility

If we voice, *tutorial please*, the demonstrator replies, in the voice of the lady *September*, and displays the text shown in the upper part of Figure A - 7, offering the choices of listing all lessons, selecting a specific lesson number, or abandoning the tutorial.

If we voice *list lessons* then *September* voices and displays details of lessons 1 – 9 as shown in the lower part of the figure.

If we select a particular lesson by voicing *lesson 1* say, then *September* echoes and displays the lesson number and its title *Lesson 1 – Examples of Use*, as shown in the upper part of Figure A - 8. This is shortly followed by *September* voicing and displaying the first sentence of this lesson i.e., *a lady has two Siamese cats, three Burmese cats, and a nervous budgie* as an example of something we can say to the demonstrator (*October*).

Shortly after, *September* reads out the example sentence to *October*. *October* echoes vocally and displays the sentence *a lady has two Siamese cats, three Burmese cats, and a nervous budgie* as shown in the upper part of Figure A - 9. This enables *September* to verify that *October* has heard it correctly.

September then confirms the correctness of the sentence by saying *ok, fine*. This causes *October* to process the sentence and, if it is found to be semantically valid, to add information derived from it to her mental model. *October* confirms understanding by adding the sentence to, and displaying it in the sentence file, and voicing and displaying the phrase *Right, I understand* as shown in the Figure A - 10.

September then invites continuing with a further example sentence by saying *Please say 'next' or 'abandon' to continue.* If we choose *next*, then the cycle just described is repeated for the next example sentence. There are typically 10 – 20 example sentences in each lesson. A proportion of the sentences test *October's* understanding of the sentences input so far. For example, a sequence of sentences input by *September* may say:

> • *A lady has two Siamese cats, three Burmese cats and a nervous budgie*
> • *Each Siamese cat has two toys and one biscuit*
> • *Each Burmese cat has one more toy and two more biscuits*
> • *The budgie has one more biscuit and one more toy*
> • *Count each lady, each cat, each toy, and each biscuit*

These will cause *October* to voice and display the reply:

> • *There is just one lady, five cats, one budgie, eight toys, and nine biscuits*

The sentences presented to *October* by *September* are predefined to illustrate the demonstrator's capability. However, *October's* responses to the sentences are generated as a result of computation and new mental model building, just as if *October* were responding to new user input.

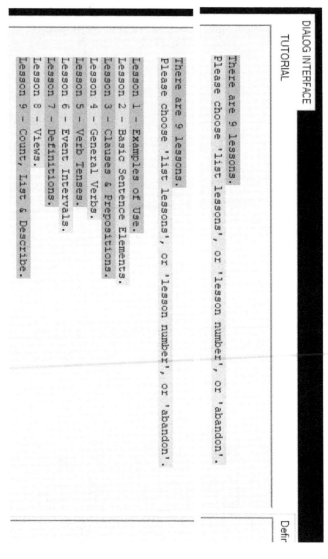

DIALOG INTERFACE

TUTORIAL

There are 9 lessons.
Please choose 'list lessons', or 'lesson number', or 'abandon'.

There are 9 lessons.
Please choose 'list lessons', or 'lesson number', or 'abandon'.

lesson 1 - Examples of Use.
lesson 2 - Basic Sentence Elements.
lesson 3 - Clauses & Prepositions.
Lesson 4 - General Verbs.
Lesson 5 - Verb Tenses.
Lesson 6 - Event Intervals.
Lesson 7 - Definitions.
Lesson 8 - Views.
Lesson 9 - Count, List & Describe.

Defir

Figure A - 7

216

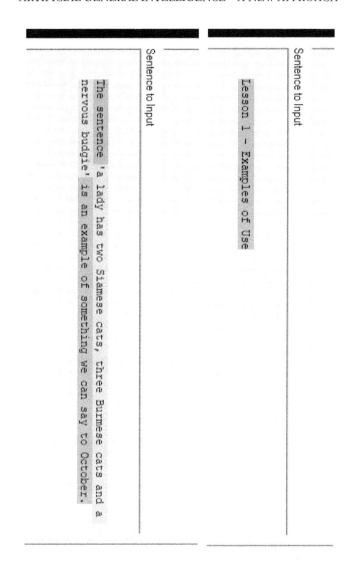

Figure A - 8

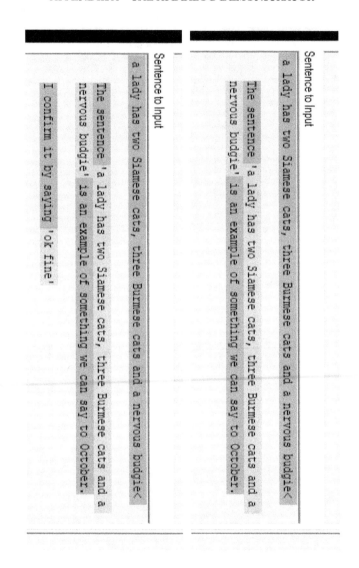

Sentence to Input

a lady has two Siamese cats, three Burmese cats and a nervous budgie<

The sentence 'a lady has two Siamese cats, three Burmese cats and a nervous budgie' is an example of something we can say to October.

Sentence to Input

a lady has two Siamese cats, three Burmese cats and a nervous budgie<

The sentence 'a lady has two Siamese cats, three Burmese cats and a nervous budgie' is an example of something we can say to October.

I confirm it by saying 'ok fine'

Figure A - 9

TUTORIAL

@1 A lady has two Siamese cats, three Burmese cats and a nervous budgie.
Right, I understand.

Def

Sentence to Input

The sentence 'a lady has two Siamese cats, three Burmese cats and a nervous budgie' is an example of something we can say to October.

Please say 'next' or 'abandon' to continue.

Figure A - 10

219

Dialog files

If we say *dialog please*, the demonstrator (*October*) speaks, and displays the text shown in the upper part of Figure A - 11, offering the choices of *list* to list all presently stored files containing dialogues, *commands* to detail available commands or *abandon*, to abandon the facility and return to the initial screen.

If we say *list* then *October* tells us of and displays all presently stored dialogue files, as shown in the lower part of the figure.

If we say *commands* then *October* tells us about and displays commands that we can use with dialogue files, being *open* to open an existing file, *reset* to clear the contents of a file, *delete* to delete a file, or *create new* to create a new file. This is shown in Figure A - 12. *October* errors if we try to apply open, reset or delete to a file which does not exist, or try to apply *create new* to one that does.

If we say *open* followed by a file name, *October* echoes and displays the command and asks us to say *ok* to confirm the operation. This is shown in Figure A - 13. Alternatively, we can say *abandon*.

Figure A - 14 shows a typical result of an *open* command, the initial screen is returned to, the dialogue file is opened, and its contents displayed. *October* rebuilds the mental model corresponding to the dialogue. At this point we can continue speaking further sentences to *October* to be added to this dialogue.

Figure A - 15 shows *reset* followed by a file name. Again, *October* echoes and displays the command and requests *ok* to confirm. In this case the initial screen is returned to but displaying the empty file; the corresponding mental model is also deleted. Again, we can continue speaking further

sentences to *October*, to build a new dialogue and model.
The command *delete* followed by a file name causes the file to be deleted. If the file deleted happens to be the current one, then the initial screen is returned to, and the *default* file is automatically opened and displayed. It is not possible to delete the *default* file and October errors if this is attempted.

Figure A - 16 shows the result of the *create new* command. The word *create* appears in the sentence input box followed by the spelling cursor. We can now dictate to *October* each letter of the file name. If a letter is misheard, we say *undo*. When the name is complete we say *ok* as shown in Figure A - 17. If we want to abandon, we say *abandon*. We can use the normal or phonetic alphabet e.g., *alpha*, *bravo*, *charlie* etc., if we want. We need to say an additional *ok* on name completion for *October* to execute the command, otherwise we can say *abandon*. The main screen is returned to with the new empty file open, ready for sentence input.

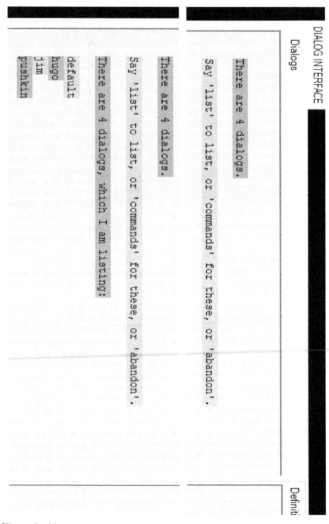

Figure A - 11

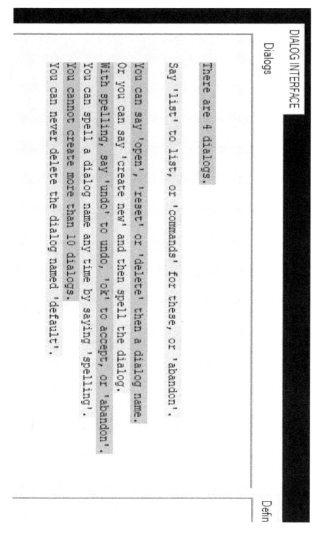

Figure A - 12

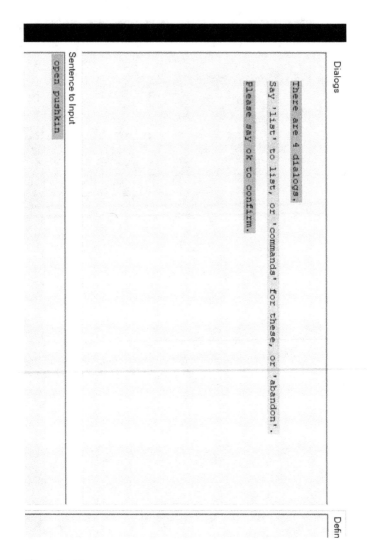

Figure A - 13

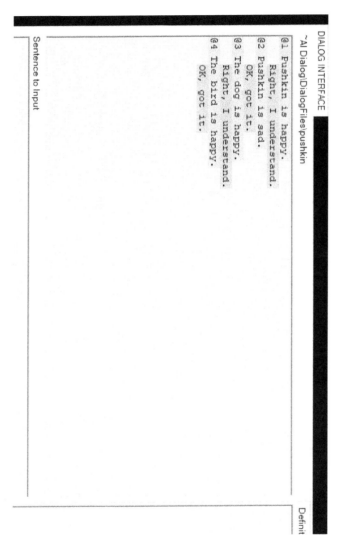

Figure A - 14

225

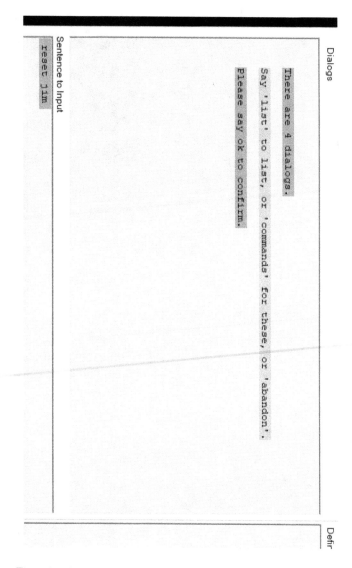

Dialogs

There are 4 dialogs.

Say 'list' to list, or 'commands' for these, or 'abandon'.

Please say ok to confirm.

Sentence to Input

reset jim

Defir

Figure A - 15

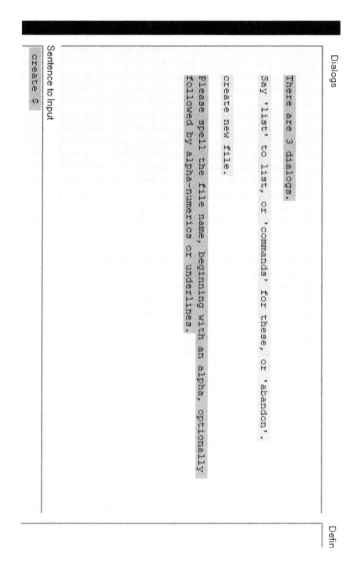

Figure A - 16

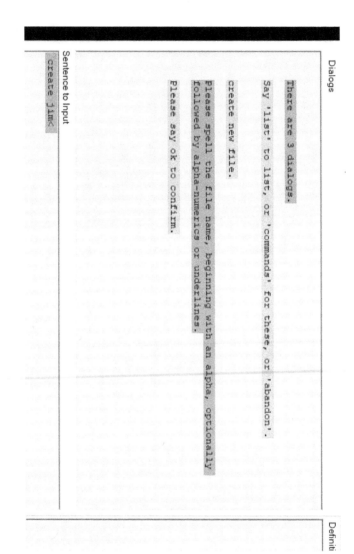

Dialogs

There are 3 dialogs.

Say 'list' to list, or 'commands' for these, or 'abandon'.

create new file.

Please spell the file name, beginning with an alpha, optionally followed by alpha-numerics or underlines.

Please say ok to confirm.

Sentence to Input

create jim<

Definiti

Figure A - 17

Help

If we say *help please*, the demonstrator (*October*) speaks, and displays the text shown in the upper part of Figure A - 18, offering the choices of help on *everything*, or a particular *topic,* or *abandon*, to abandon the facility and return to the initial screen.

If we say *topic* then as shown in the centre part of the figure, *October* tells us of and displays all possible topics, being *sentence, edit, position, punctuation, case, spelling, undo, dialog, tutorial, tips*, or *abandon,* to abandon the facility and return to the initial screen.

Sentence

If we say *sentence*, *October* speaks and displays the text shown in the lower part of the figure showing how a new sentence may be input to the demonstrator (*October*), and how *October* echoes the sentence so you can verify it, and how you can respond with *ok, fine* to cause *October* to act on it.

The upper part of Figure A - 18 shows how you can alternatively *abandon* the sentence if it is wrong. The second part of the figure mentions how you can alternatively *edit* the sentence prior to inputting it again. This is the subject of the *edit* topic, which the demonstrator (*October*) allows us to select if we wish.

Edit

If we say *edit* at this point, *October* describes the edit facilities, beginning with the *don't say* command, shown in the lower part of Figure A - 19, which, followed by an existing sentence phrase, enables us to delete erroneous text at a specified position within a sentence. Similarly, the *please say* command, shown in the Figure A - 20 followed by a new phrase, enables us to insert that phrase at a specified position within a sentence. Choosing an edit position within a sentence is the subject of the *position* help.

Position

help position shows you can choose an edit position within a sentence by saying *after* or *before*, followed by a sentence phrase. This is illustrated in Figure A - 21. Variants of these commands allow use of the keywords *next* or *previous* e.g., *after next* or *before previous*, shown in the lower part of the figure.

Punctuation

help punctuation shows you can choose an edit position within a sentence and add punctuation. This is illustrated in Figure A - 22. So, you can say *comma* or *semicolon* or *colon* or *quote* after having chosen a sentence position. By saying *space*, you can remove punctuation, as the figure shows. You can also say *possessive* to change, for example, *cat* to *cat's*.

Case

help case shows that having chosen a position before a particular word in a sentence, you can change the case of the first letter of the word, as shown in the upper part of Figure A - 23. Alternatively, you can change the case of the whole word, as shown in the lower part of the figure.

Spelling

help spelling shows that having chosen a position in a sentence you can spell a new word at this position by saying *spelling*. This is shown in the upper two parts of Figure A - 24. The second part shows that a spelling cursor $ appears at the chosen position. We can then spell out each individual letter e.g., *a, b, c,* and so on. The lower part of the figure shows the word progressively building up.

Alternatively, as shown in the upper part of Figure A - 25 we can use the phonetic alphabet e.g., *alpha, bravo, charlie,* and so on. If we make a mistake, we can say *undo,* and the letter is removed. We can say *undo* as often as we like. As shown in the centre part of the figure, we can spell digits by saying e.g., *one, two, three,* and so on, or alternatively *digit one, digit two, digit three,* and so on. When the spelling is complete, we say *ok* and the spelling cursor is removed, but the new word remains as described in the lower part of the figure. *October* repeats the word to you. Alternatively, if we wish to abandon spelling we can say *abandon.*

Undo

help undo shows that we can undo a sentence edit by saying *undo.* This is illustrated in upper part of Figure A - 26. The second part of the figure shows that we can say *undo* as often as we like, right up to the initial input. The lower part of the figure shows that we can say *redo* to reverse the effect of an *undo.* Again, we can say *redo* as often as we like, up to the final edit.

Dialog and tutorial

help dialog and *help tutorial* respectively, describe the dialog file facilities and the tutorial facilities as already covered in sections *Dialog files* and *Tutorial facility.*

Tips

help tips describes one or two tips associated with user input, and sentences resulting from this, as shown in Figure A - 27.

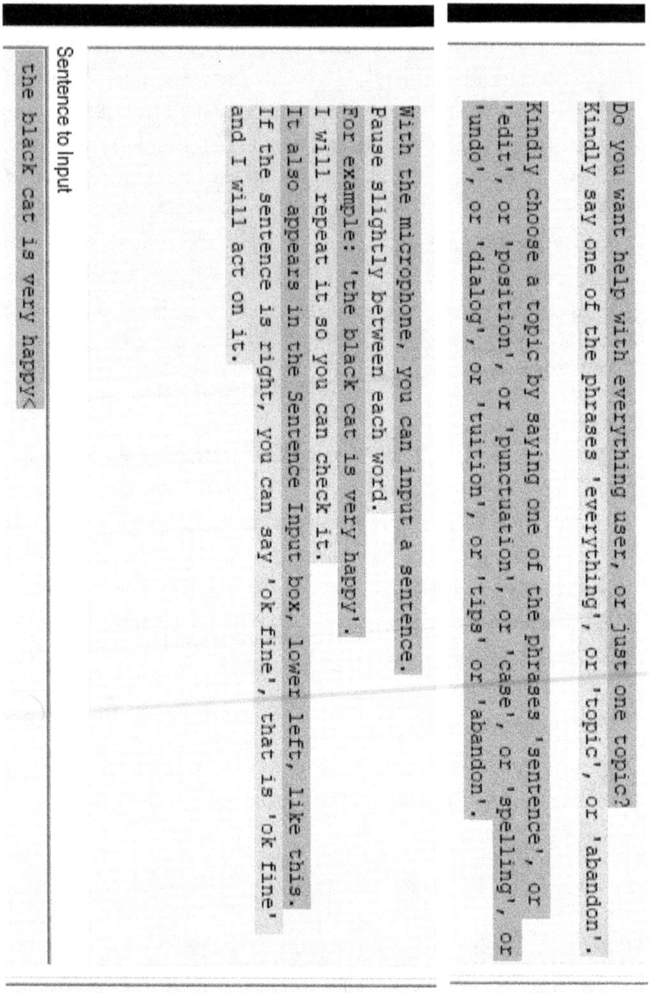

Do you want help with everything user, or just one topic?
Kindly say one of the phrases 'everything', or 'topic', or 'abandon'.

Kindly choose a topic by saying one of the phrases 'sentence', or 'edit', or 'position', or 'punctuation', or 'case', or 'spelling', or 'undo', or 'dialog', or 'tuition', or 'tips' or 'abandon'.

With the microphone, you can input a sentence.
Pause slightly between each word.
For example: 'the black cat is very happy'.
I will repeat it so you can check it.
It also appears in the Sentence Input box, lower left, like this.
If the sentence is right, you can say 'ok fine', that is 'ok fine'
and I will act on it.

Sentence to Input

the black cat is very happy<

Figure A - 18

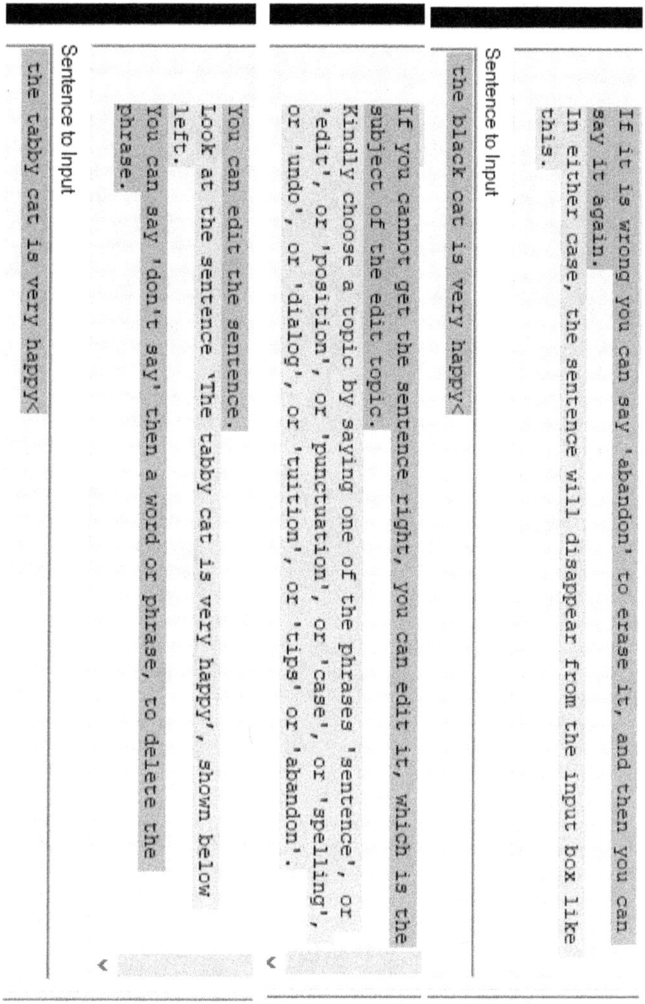

Sentence to Input

If it is wrong you can say 'abandon' to erase it, and then you can say it again.
In either case, the sentence will disappear from the input box like this.

Sentence to Input

the black cat is very happy<

If you cannot get the sentence right, you can edit it, which is the subject of the edit topic.
Kindly choose a topic by saying one of the phrases 'sentence', or 'edit', or 'position', or 'punctuation', or 'case', or 'spelling', or 'undo', or 'dialog', or 'tuition', or 'tips' or 'abandon'.

Sentence to Input

You can edit the sentence.
Look at the sentence 'The tabby cat is very happy', shown below left.
You can say 'don't say' then a word or phrase, to delete the phrase.

the tabby cat is very happy<

Figure A - 19

233

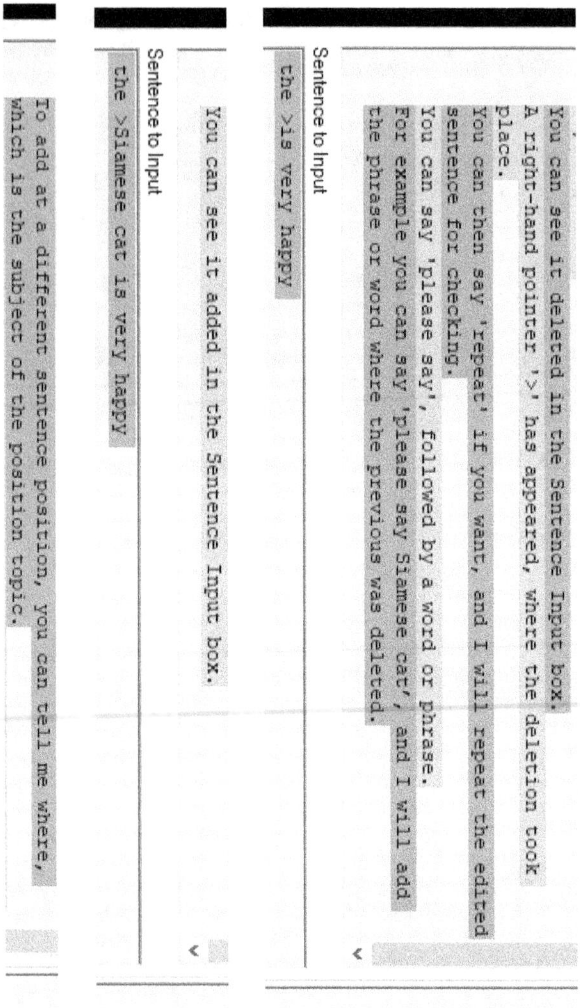

You can see it deleted in the Sentence Input box.
A right-hand pointer '>' has appeared, where the deletion took place.
You can then say 'repeat' if you want, and I will repeat the edited sentence for checking.
You can say 'please say', followed by a word or phrase.
For example you can say 'please say Siamese cat', and I will add the phrase or word where the previous was deleted.

Sentence to Input

the >is very happy

You can see it added in the Sentence Input box.

Sentence to Input

the >Siamese cat is very happy

To add at a different sentence position, you can tell me where, which is the subject of the position topic.

Figure A - 20

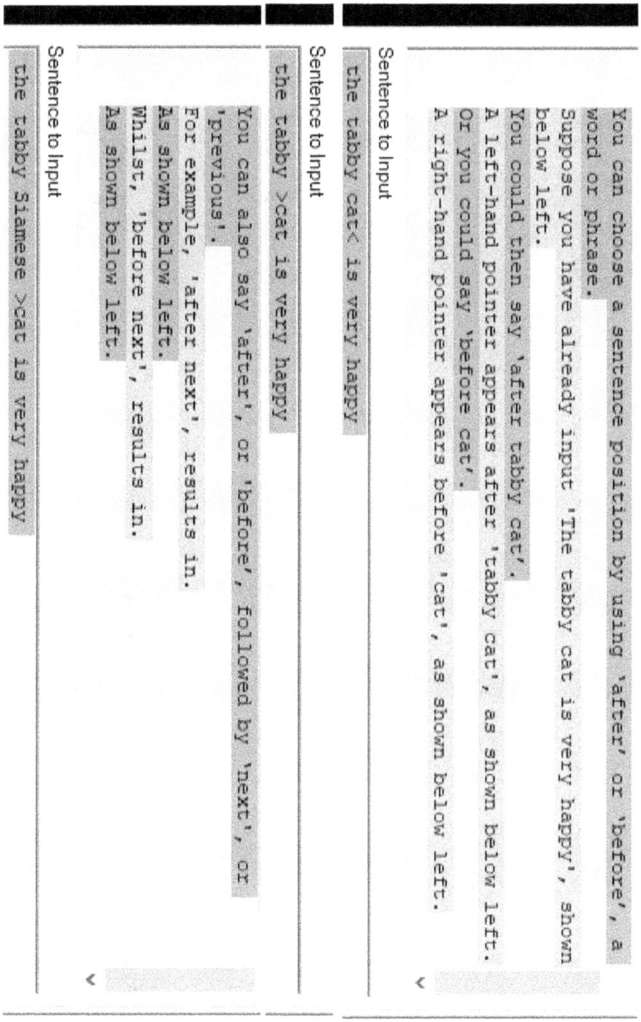

Sentence to Input

the tabby cat< is very happy

You can choose a sentence position by using 'after' or 'before', a word or phrase.
Suppose you have already input 'The tabby cat is very happy', shown below left.
You could then say 'after tabby cat'.
A left-hand pointer appears after 'tabby cat', as shown below left.
Or you could say 'before cat'.
A right-hand pointer appears before 'cat', as shown below left.

Sentence to Input

the tabby >cat is very happy

Sentence to Input

You can also say 'after', or 'before', followed by 'next', or 'previous'.
For example, 'after next', results in.
As shown below left.
Whilst, 'before next', results in.
As shown below left.

Sentence to Input

the tabby Siamese >cat is very happy

Figure A - 21

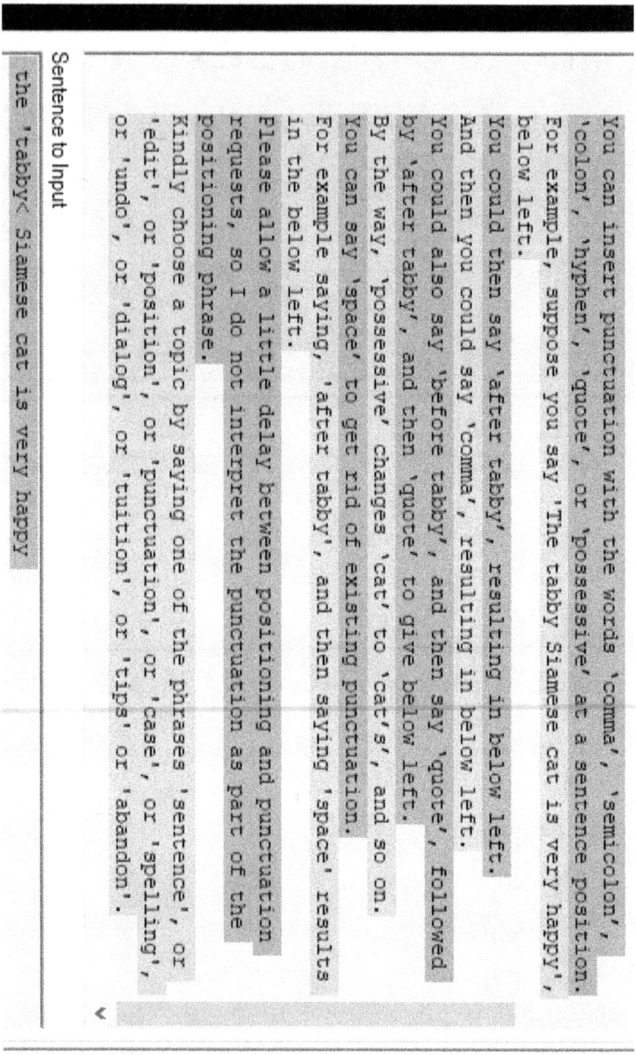

You can insert punctuation with the words 'comma', 'semicolon', 'colon', 'hyphen', 'quote', or 'possessive' at a sentence position. For example, suppose you say 'The tabby Siamese cat is very happy', below left.

You could then say 'after tabby', resulting in below left. And then you could say 'comma', resulting in below left. You could also say 'before tabby', and then say 'quote', followed by 'after tabby', and then 'quote' to give below left.

By the way, 'possessive' changes 'cat' to 'cat's', and so on.

You can say 'space' to get rid of existing punctuation. For example saying, 'after tabby', and then saying 'space' results in the below left.

Please allow a little delay between positioning and punctuation requests, so I do not interpret the punctuation as part of the positioning phrase.

Kindly choose a topic by saying one of the phrases 'sentence', or 'edit', or 'position', or 'punctuation', or 'case', or 'spelling', or 'undo', or 'dialog', or 'tuition', or 'tips' or 'abandon'.

Sentence to Input

the 'tabby< Siamese cat is very happy

Figure A - 22

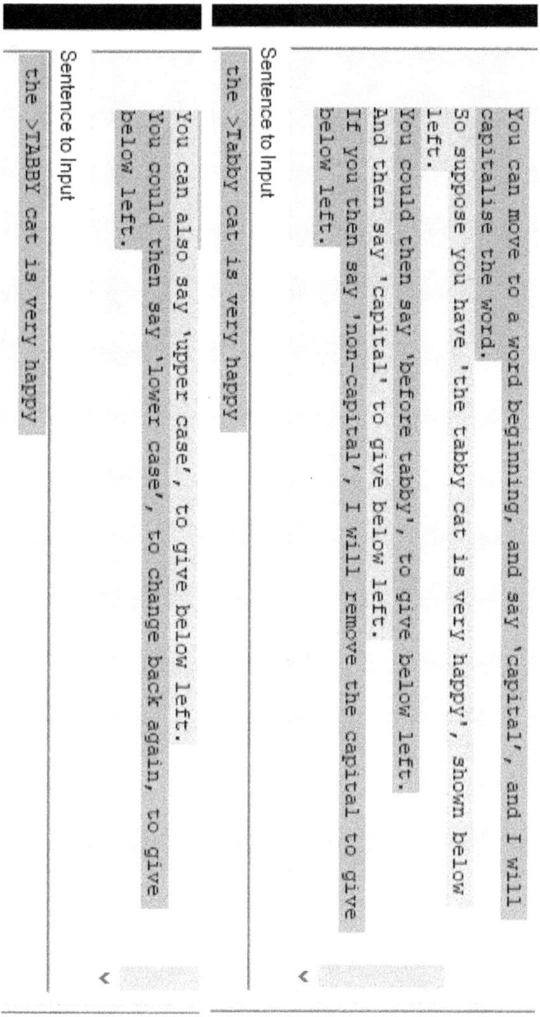

You can move to a word beginning, and say 'capital', and I will capitalise the word.
So suppose you have 'the tabby cat is very happy', shown below left.
You could then say 'before tabby', to give below left.
And then say 'capital' to give below left.
If you then say 'non-capital', I will remove the capital to give below left.

Sentence to Input

the >Tabby cat is very happy

You can also say 'upper case', to give below left.
You could then say 'lower case', to change back again, to give below left.

Sentence to Input

the >TABBY cat is very happy

Figure A - 23

237

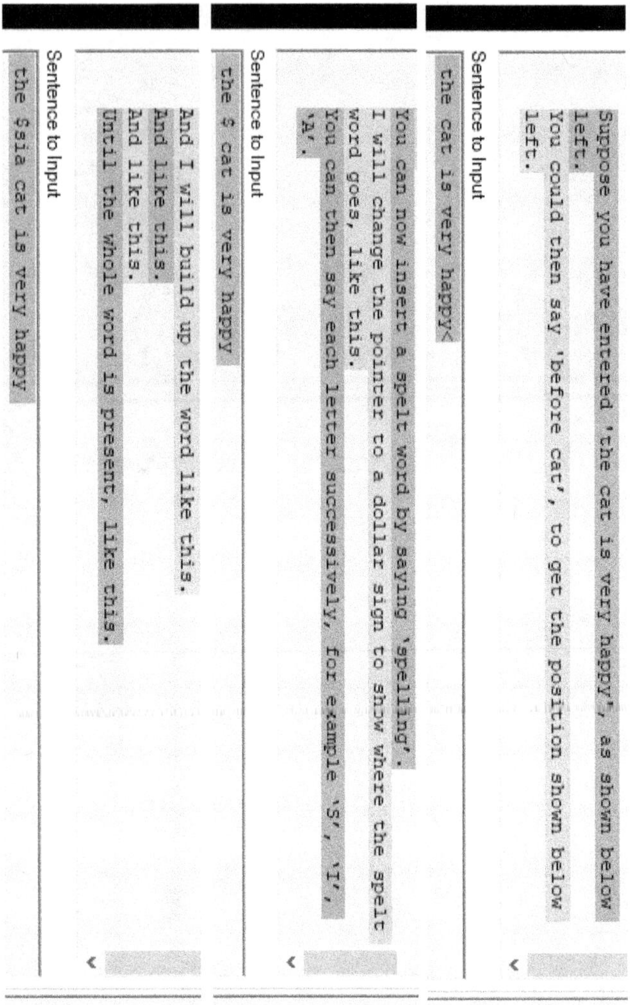

Sentence to Input

the cat is very happy

Suppose you have entered 'the cat is very happy', as shown below left.
You could then say 'before cat', to get the position shown below left.

Sentence to Input

the $ cat is very happy

You can now insert a spelt word by saying 'spelling'.
I will change the pointer to a dollar sign to show where the spelt word goes, like this.
You can then say each letter successively, for example 'S', 'I', 'A'.

Sentence to Input

the $sia cat is very happy

And I will build up the word like this.
And like this.
And like this.
Until the whole word is present, like this.

Figure A - 24

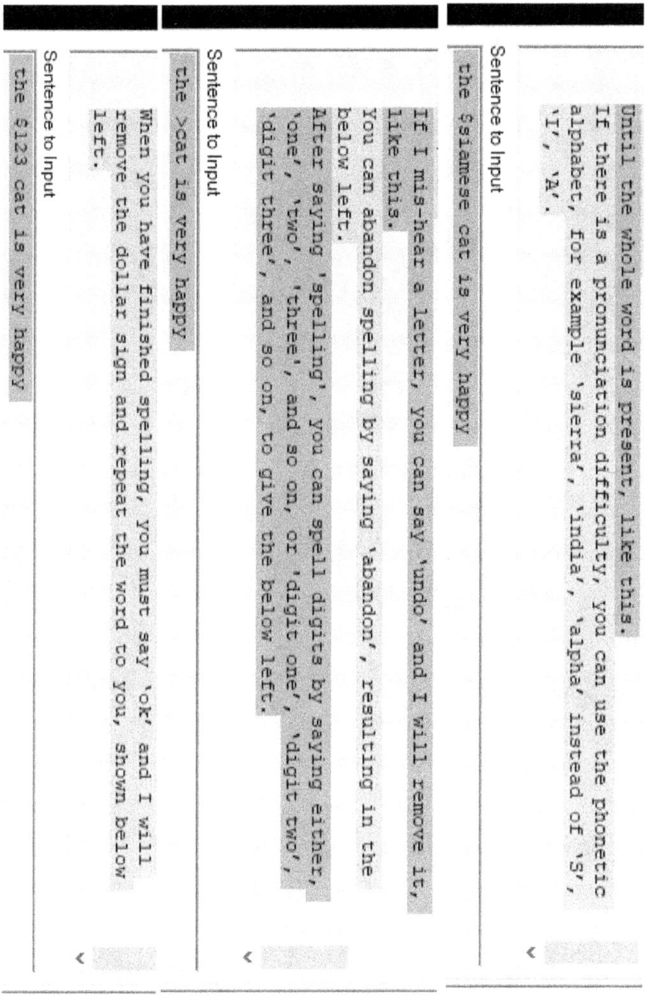

Until the whole word is present, like this.
If there is a pronunciation difficulty, you can use the phonetic alphabet, for example 'sierra', 'india', 'alpha' instead of 'S', 'I', 'A'.

Sentence to Input
the §siamese cat is very happy

If I mis-hear a letter, you can say 'undo' and I will remove it, like this.
You can abandon spelling by saying 'abandon', resulting in the below left.
After saying 'spelling', you can spell digits by saying either, 'one', 'two', 'three', and so on, or 'digit one', 'digit two', 'digit three', and so on, to give the below left.

Sentence to Input
the >cat is very happy

When you have finished spelling, you must say 'ok' and I will remove the dollar sign and repeat the word to you, shown below left.

Sentence to Input
the $123 cat is very happy

Figure A - 25

239

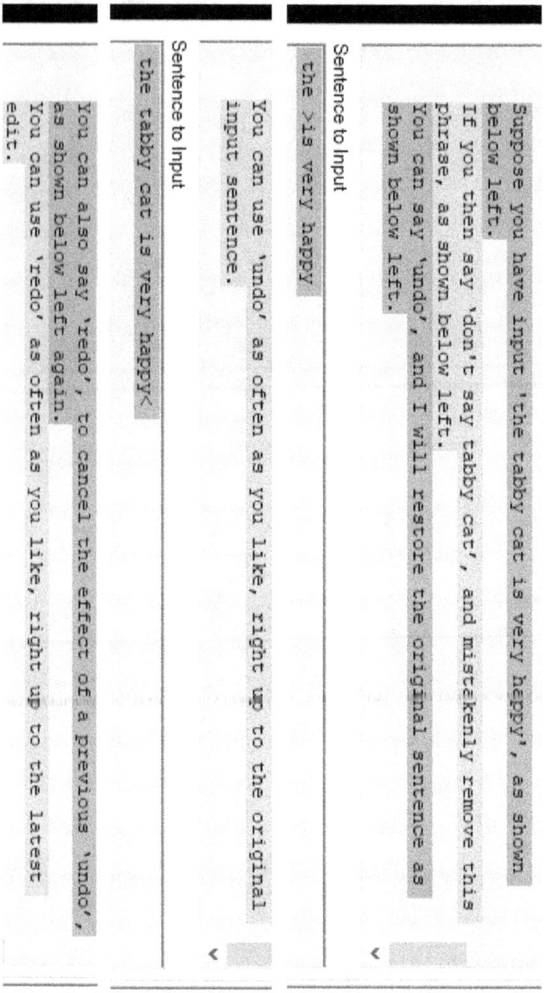

Suppose you have input 'the tabby cat is very happy', as shown
below left.
If you then say 'don't say tabby cat', and mistakenly remove this
phrase, as shown below left.
You can say 'undo', and I will restore the original sentence as
shown below left.

Sentence to Input

the >is very happy

You can use 'undo' as often as you like, right up to the original
input sentence.

Sentence to Input

the tabby cat is very happy<

You can also say 'redo', to cancel the effect of a previous 'undo',
as shown below left again.
You can use 'redo' as often as you like, right up to the latest
edit.

Figure A - 26

At any time, you can say 'repeat', and I will repeat the sentence for you to check.

If you request something not sensible, I will ignore it and say 'I don't think so'.

If I mis-hear you, I will say 'Say again please'.

There is no need to start a sentence with a capital and end it with a period, as I add these when a sentence is accepted after you say 'ok', 'ok'.

Ordinals, for example 22nd or 34th, as they appear in the Sentence Input box, are automatically converted by me to the form hash 22 or hash 34, following 'ok', 'ok'.

.

So there is no need to edit them into this form.

Figure A - 27

Text mode

We move on now to Text mode. Figure A - 28 shows the result of clicking *Tutorial*. The box heading changes to *No file selected* and one of a series of lessons may be selected by the user from the drop-down list.

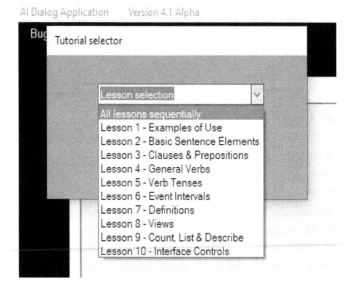

Figure A - 28

Figure A - 29 shows the tutorial facility in action after *Lesson 1 – Examples of Use* has been selected. The tutorial facility automatically presents the user with sentences one at a time in the *Sentence to Input* box, together with an invitation to click *Enter* to submit the sentence to the demonstrator, and then to click *Next* to get the next sentence. If the demonstrator understands the sentence, it repeats it in the top left conversation box, together with its response e.g. *A lady has two Siamese cats, three Burmese cats and a nervous budgie* is input, and the demonstrator responds with *Right, I understand.* The input sentence is shown in light blue, and the demonstrator's response is inset in light red. Each sentence is automatically numbered.

The figure shows that successive data sentences:

• *A lady has two Siamese cats, three Burmese cats and a nervous budgie*
• *Each Siamese cat has two toys and one biscuit*
• *Each Burmese cat has one more toy and two more biscuits*
• *The budgie has one more biscuit and one more toy*

have already been input to the demonstrator, and that the tutorial facility has readied the sentence *Count each lady, each cat, each toy, and each biscuit* for input.

Figure A - 30 shows the result of clicking *Enter*. The demonstrator recognises the request, consults its mental model, does some deduction, and responds with *There is just one lady, five cats, one budgie, eight toys, and nine biscuits.*

All of the tutorial examples, showing user input and demonstrator response are listed in the sections numbered *Lesson 1* to *Lesson 10*, in *Appendix B - AI Dialog Lessons* following this appendix.

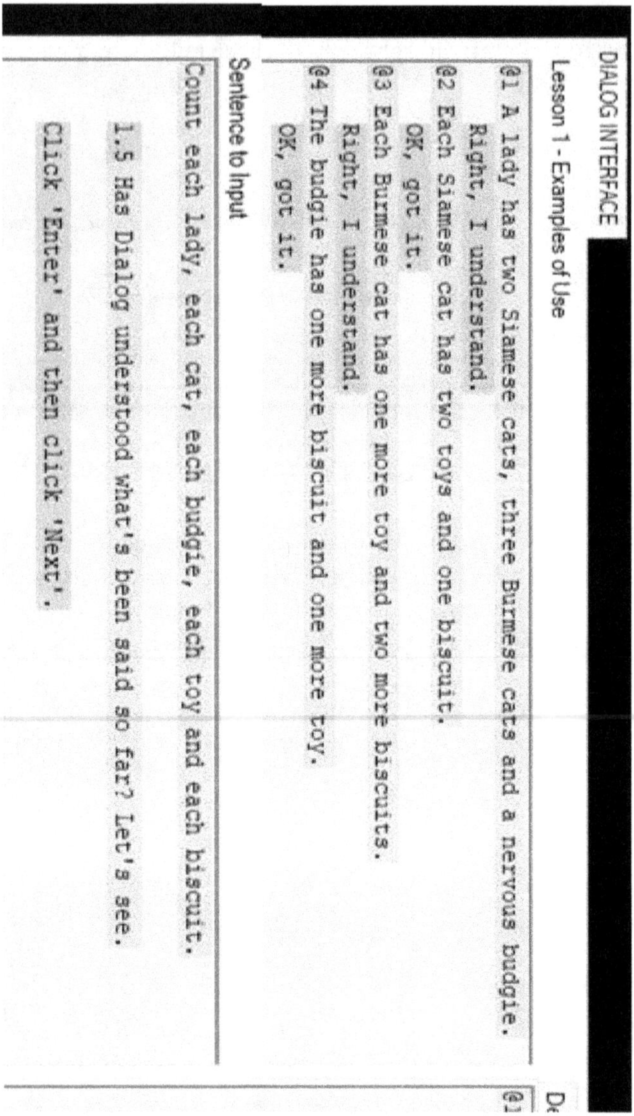

DIALOG INTERFACE

Lesson 1 - Examples of Use

@1 A lady has two Siamese cats, three Burmese cats and a nervous budgie.
   Right, I understand.

@2 Each Siamese cat has two toys and one biscuit.
   OK, got it.

@3 Each Burmese cat has one more toy and two more biscuits.
   Right, I understand.

@4 The budgie has one more biscuit and one more toy.
   OK, got it.

Sentence to Input

Count each lady, each cat, each budgie, each toy and each biscuit.

1.5 Has Dialog understood what's been said so far? Let's see.

Click 'Enter' and then click 'Next'.

De

@1

Figure A - 29

244

DIALOG INTERFACE

Lesson 1 - Examples of Use

Q1 A lady has two Siamese cats, three Burmese cats and a nervous budgie.
Right, I understand.

Q2 Each Siamese cat has two toys and one biscuit.
OK, got it.

Q3 Each Burmese cat has one more toy and two more biscuits.
Right, I understand.

Q4 The budgie has one more biscuit and one more toy.
OK, got it.

Q5 Count each lady, each cat, each budgie, each toy and each biscuit.
There is just one lady, five cats, one budgie, eight toys, and nine biscuits.

Figure A - 30

Mental Model tab

Figure A - 31 shows the content of the Mental Model tab following input of the first few tutorial sentences. This shows the portion of the mental model represented by the sentence *A lady has two Siamese cats, three Burmese cats and a nervous budgie.*

The demonstrator has added instances to the model, representing the *lady*, the adjective *Siamese* (2 instances), the adjective *Burmese* (3 instances), the adjective *nervous* and a total of five *cat* instances representing each *cat*, and one *budgie* instance. The instance concept and how the demonstrator uses it has been explained earlier in the book.

The demonstrator has then added *is* and *has* relations, connecting the instances together, to represent the semantics of the sentence. So, we have *cat (1) is Siamese (1), lady (1) has cat (1)* and so on. The prefix to each of these of *present[0] ->* indicates that the relation is in the present tense (since the demonstrator can handle past, present, and future tenses) and the event interval *[0]* flags the first of a sequence, as the demonstrator supports sequences of events.

Count and *List*

The earlier examples of Figure A - 29 and Figure A - 30 showed that by consulting the mental model, the demonstrator could do some mental arithmetic and count things. Figure A - 32 shows the demonstrator consulting the mental model and performing some logic, rather than arithmetic.

Definitions	Subvocalisation	Mental Model

```
@1 A lady has two Siamese cats, three

new inst.. lady(1)
new inst.. cat(1)
new inst.. Siamese(1)
new inst.. cat(2)
new inst.. Siamese(2)
new inst.. cat(3)
new inst.. Burmese(1)
new inst.. cat(4)
new inst.. Burmese(2)
new inst.. cat(5)
new inst.. Burmese(3)
new inst.. budgie(1)
new inst.. nervous(1)

present[0]-> cat(1) is Siamese(1)
present[0]-> lady(1) has cat(1)
present[0]-> cat(2) is Siamese(2)
present[0]-> lady(1) has cat(2)
present[0]-> cat(3) is Burmese(1)
present[0]-> lady(1) has cat(3)
present[0]-> cat(4) is Burmese(2)
present[0]-> lady(1) has cat(4)
present[0]-> cat(5) is Burmese(3)
present[0]-> lady(1) has cat(5)
present[0]-> budgie(1) is nervous(1)
present[0]-> lady(1) has budgie(1)
```

Figure A - 31

DIALOG INTERFACE

Lesson 1 - Examples of Use

@6 Jack, Humpty and Georgie each likes Jill.

Right, I understand.

@7 Jill likes Jack, Georgie and Cole.

OK, got it.

@8 List each person that likes Jill.

There is: Jack that is liking Jill; Humpty that is liking Jill; and
Georgie that is liking Jill.

@9 List each person that Jill likes.

There is: Jack that Jill is liking; Georgie that Jill is liking;
and Cole that Jill is liking.

@10 List each person that Jill likes, that likes Jill.

There is: Jack that Jill is liking, that is liking Jill; and
Georgie that Jill is liking, that is liking Jill.

@11 Describe the budgie.

There is just one budgie. Viewing the budgie. The budgie is
nervous. The budgie has a biscuit, and a toy. Leaving the budgie.

@12 Every animal that is fretful does a medial dread. A bird and

Figure A - 32

248

Definitions

Figure A - 33 shows the *definition* sentence *Every person that is a doctor: has a medical degree; is kind and compassionate* being input, with the demonstrator's response of *Fine, I'll remember that definition*, and the corresponding content of the *Definitions* tab. The data sentence *Tom is a doctor* is then input and Figure A - 34 shows the content of the Mental Model tab following this input.

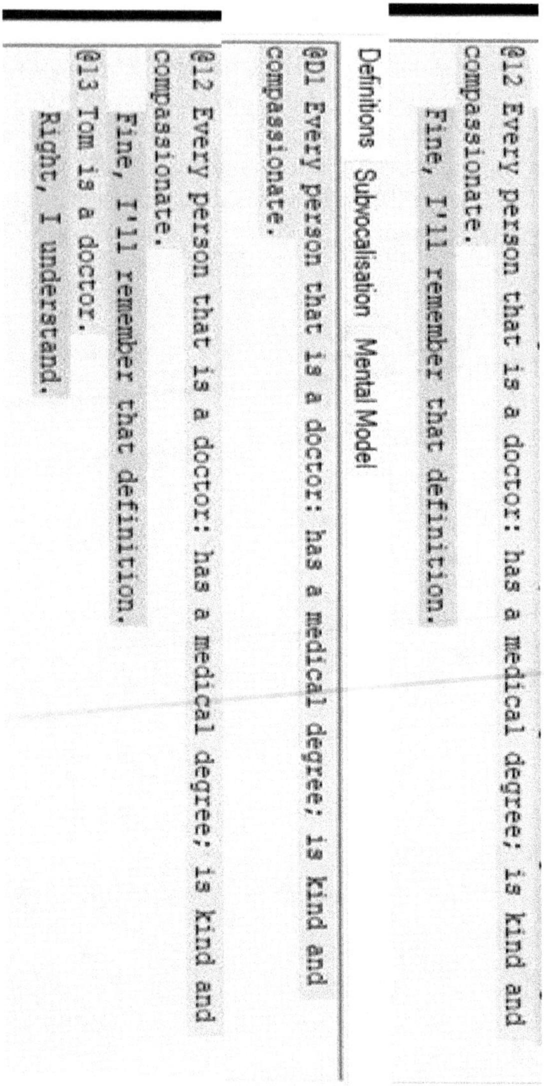

@12 Every person that is a doctor: has a medical degree; is kind and
compassionate.

   Fine, I'll remember that definition.

Definitions   Subvocalisation   Mental Model

@D1 Every person that is a doctor: has a medical degree; is kind and
compassionate.

@12 Every person that is a doctor: has a medical degree; is kind and
compassionate.

   Fine, I'll remember that definition.

@13 Tom is a doctor.
   Right, I understand.

Figure A - 33

250

```
@13 Tom is a doctor.

new inst.. Tom(1)
new inst.. doctor(1)
new inst.. %instance(1)

present[0]-> doctor(1) is %instance(1)
present[0]-> Tom(1) is doctor(1)

    @D1.1 Every person that is a doctor has a medical degree.

new inst.. degree(1)
new inst.. medical(1)

present[0]-> degree(1) is medical(1)
present[0]->~Tom(1) has degree(1)

    @D1.2 Every person that is a doctor is kind and compassionate.

new inst.. kind(1)
new inst.. compassionate(1)

present[0]->~Tom(1) is kind(1)
present[0]->~Tom(1) is compassionate(1)
```

Figure A - 34

251

Describe and subvocalisation

Figure A - 35 shows input of the *describe* sentence *describe Tom* and the demonstrator's response to this. Figure A - 36 shows the *Subvocalisation* tab reflecting the demonstrator's logical processes as it forms the multi-sentence reply.

Text files

If you click the *New - Reset* pushbutton, the window shown in Figure A - 37 appears allowing you to create a new text file (*sentence test 1* – in the example) in which to record a new conversation with the demonstrator. Alternatively, you can reset or clear the contents of an existing file by choosing an existing file name.

If you click the *Open* pushbutton, a similar window appears, but allowing you to recall a previous conversation with the demonstrator. The demonstrator will load the associated file into the conversation window replacing any earlier conversation file, but retaining its contents, and rebuild the mental model associated with the new file.

If you click the *Delete* pushbutton a similar window appears, but allowing you to delete any existing conversation file. However, you cannot delete the *default* file. If you delete the file which is presently open, it is automatically replaced with the *default* file, and the mental model is rebuilt from this.

If the demonstrator is closed by clicking the *Exit* pushbutton, on restarting the demonstrator, any previously open conversation text file is automatically reopened, and the mental model rebuilt from it, so you can carry on working with it.

Errors

If a sentence is input which the demonstrator does not understand, an error report appears in the *Sentence to Input* box as shown in Figure A - 38. Before you can carry on you must click the *Got it* pushbutton. The sentence can then be revised and re-input.

Q12 Every person that is a doctor; has a medical degree; is kind and
compassionate.

Fine, I'll remember that definition.

Q13 Tom is a doctor.

Right, I understand.

Q14 Describe Tom.

There is just one Tom. Viewing Tom. Tom is a doctor, kind, and
compassionate. Tom has a degree. Viewing the degree. The degree is
medical. Leaving the degree. Leaving Tom.

Figure A - 35

@14 Describe Tom.

Definitions   Subvocalisation   Mental Model

'There is just one Tom.'
Viewing Tom.
List each x that Tom is.
There is: a doctor that Tom is; kind that Tom is; and compassionate
that Tom is.
• Tom is a doctor, kind, and compassionate.'
      Viewing the doctor.
      List each x that has the doctor.
      List each x that the doctor is.
      List each x that the doctor has.
      Leaving the doctor.
      Viewing the kind.
      List each x that has the kind.
      List each x that the kind is.
      List each x that the kind has.
      Leaving the kind.
      Viewing the compassionate.
      List each x that has the compassionate.
      List each x that the compassionate is.
      List each x that the compassionate is.

Figure A - 36

255

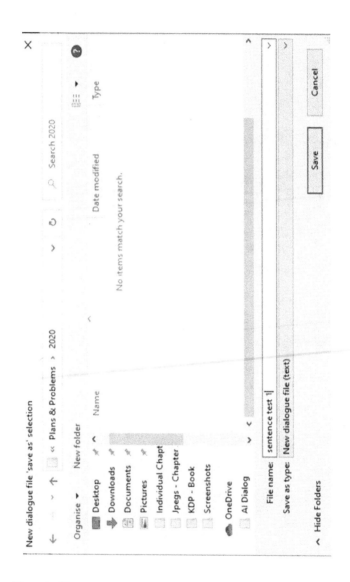

Figure A - 37

Figure A - 38

Projected developments

The following bulleted sections indicate where, at the time of writing, demonstrator software development is planned to enhance capability.

• Quantifiers of countable and uncountable *instances*; countable *instances* are to be flagged as *integer*, retaining *quantity* for uncountables, enabling plural elimination

• Unknowns; *person, thing* and other unknowns are to be allowed in objects/complements as well as subjects

• Verb passive forms are to be added; requiring *<verb, third person present tense>* transformation using *is <verb, third person past tense> by,* see (Seely, Passive voice, 2004), allowing expressions like *the hill is climbed by Jack*

• Verb infinitive forms are to be added; for example, *Jack likes to tease Jill* using the infinitive form *to tease*

• *Describe;* at present, the output is naïve and is to be more sophisticated; *Describe* cannot cope with some data structures and requires extension

• Logical operators; are to be extended to encompass inclusive and exclusive *or* functions; canonical sum-of-products, or product-of-sums forms (Subramyam, 2005)

• Comparators are to be added; for example, *Jack is taller than Jill* or *the pen is mightier than the sword*

• Assertions are to be added; for example, *Jack is climbing!,* with response *true* or *false*

• Definitions are to be enhanced; the format is to be changed from, e*very person/thing … that is … : has …; has …; is …; is …; and is …* to, *every person/thing … that is x …, that is y … implies that: the person/thing has …; the person/thing is ..; the x has …; the x is …; the y has …; the y is …; and the y is …* this is to facilitate expressions like *every x that is greater than a y implies that: the y is less than the x*

Developments on contexts and network nodes

In the *Part II* section *Contexts and network nodes*, we showed how the introduction of nodes which were able to contain entire semantic networks provided possible solutions to many problems including representation and manipulation of

- • verb tenses
- • reported speech and thoughts
- • definitions
- • sequences of events

Semantic networks associated with these functions show a need to be contained in a separate context and network node to prevent any logic carried out on them from being mixed up with logic carried out in other contexts.

We pointed out in the same section some of the implications in regard to isomorphic subgraph searches. Development of software capable of tackling these problems is in progress.

Conclusion

Hopefully, this has given you an outline of the operation of the *AI Dialog* demonstrator, to help make the theory description of the earlier sections more real and meaningful.

(This page is intentionally blank)

APPENDIX B

AI DIALOG LESSONS

All of the tutorial examples, showing user input and demonstrator response are listed in the sections numbered *Lesson 1* to *Lesson 10*, in this appendix.

Lesson 1 - Examples of Use

1.1 Let's tell Dialog something.
A lady has two Siamese cats, three Burmese cats and a nervous budgie.

1.2 And something more.
Each Siamese cat has two toys and one biscuit.

1.3 And yet more.
Each Burmese cat has one more toy and two more biscuits.

1.4 And even more.
The budgie has one more biscuit and one more toy.

1.5 Has Dialog understood what's been said so far? Let's see.
Count each lady, each cat, each budgie, each toy, and each biscuit.
There is just one lady, five cats, one budgie, eight toys, and nine biscuits.

1.6 Let's try something else.
Jack, Humpty and Georgie each likes Jill.

1.7 And something more.
Jill likes Jack, Georgie, and Cole.

1.8 Now let's try this.
List each person that likes Jill.
There is: Jack that is liking Jill; Humpty that is liking Jill; and Georgie that is liking Jill.

1.9 And then this.
List each person that Jill likes.
There is: Jack that Jill is liking; Georgie that Jill is liking; and Cole that Jill is liking.

1.10 And something a bit more complicated.
List each person that Jill likes, that likes Jill.
There is: Jack that Jill is liking, that is liking Jill; and Georgie that Jill is liking, that is liking Jill.

1.11 Let's try this. <Describe> is very slow, be patient.
Describe the budgie.
There is just one budgie. Viewing the budgie. The budgie is nervous. The budgie has a biscuit, and a toy. Leaving the budgie.

1.12 Now something a bit more complicated again.
Every person that is a doctor: has a medical degree; is kind and compassionate.

1.13 Now this.
Tom is a doctor.

1.14 And finally this. <Describe> is very very slow, be very patient.
Describe Tom.

There is just one Tom. Viewing Tom. Tom is a doctor, kind, and compassionate. Tom has a degree. Viewing the degree. The degree is medical. Leaving the degree. Leaving Tom.

Lesson 2 - Basic Sentence Elements

2.1 Every sentence begins with a capital and ends with a stop. A simple sentence has a subject <the dog>, a verb <has> and an object <a bone>. The article <a (or an)> adds a new <instance> i.e., <dog> or <bone>. The article <the> may be used instead of <a (or an)> if <dog> or <bone> do not already exist.
A dog has a bone.

2.2 The article <the> is used here to refer to an existing <instance> <dog>. The <verb> is <is>.
The dog is happy.

2.3 The article <another> is used to add a further <dog>. The sentence <A dog is excited> would be errored as ambiguous at this stage.
Another dog is excited.

2.4 A cardinal such as <two> is used to add multiple <instances><cats> and <toys>. The verb phrase <each has> is used since plural verbs are not allowed. Cardinals beyond <nine> are expressed using an integer e.g., <There are 25 records.> making use of a <There are (or is) etc.> expression to add one or more <instances>.
Two cats each has two toys.

2.5 The word <more> must be used with <two> to add further <cats> or an error results. The phrase <another cat> could be used to add a single <cat>. The verb phrase <each is> avoids the prohibited plural verb <are>.
Two more cats each is fierce.

2.6 The article <each> enables us to refer to all existing <cat> <instances> and associates <black> with each <cat>.
Each cat is black.

2.7 The ordinal <third> selects the third <cat> out of the existing ones and associates <Siamese> with it. Ordinals beyond the ninth are expressed using <#> and an integer e.g., <The #23 cat etc.>.
The third cat is Siamese.

2.8 We can put an <adjective/adverb list> before a <subject> <parrot> or <object> <rude>. Here, <bright> qualifies <green> and <green> qualifies <parrot> and not <noisy>, because of the following comma. Then <noisy> qualifies <parrot> too. Commas in the right positions are vitally necessary. The adverb <very> then qualifies <happy>.
The bright green, noisy parrot is very happy.

2.9 Capitalised adjectives <Australian> automatically stand alone, as if bracketed by commas, and directly qualify the <object>. Do not use commas either side of them, or Dialog may either misinterpret the sentence or raise an error.
The very noisy Australian grey parrot is very sad.

2.10 We can have a <subject list> <dog>, <cat> and <parrot>, and an <object list> <toy>, <biscuit> and <owner>. The <subjects> and <objects> are separated by commas or <and> or both.
Another dog, another cat, and another parrot each has another toy, a biscuit, and an owner.

2.11 Proper nouns e.g., <London> begin with a capital letter. Phrases within single quotes <'> are treated as proper nouns, as are abbreviations e.g., <TFL>. Proper nouns

behave just as if <the> preceded them.
London has 'London Underground' and TFL.

2.12 A sentence is allowed to begin with <^> instead of a capital, to show that the first word is not a proper noun.
^influenza is infectious.

2.13 Finally, a declarative sentence using <There are ...> or <There is ...> may be used to add one or a number of new instances.
There are three very large, iced buns.

Lesson 3 – Clauses

3.1 Each <subject> or <object> contains clauses. In the <subject>, <the balloon> is the <main clause>, and <of the boy>, <with the broken leg> and <with the string> are <subsidiary clauses>. In the <object>, <dark red> is the <main clause>. The comma before <with the string> makes it apply to <balloon> and not <leg>. Commas are vital in clause lists.
The balloon of the boy with the broken leg, with the string is dark red.

3.2 Every <Form 1> <subsidiary clause> begins with one of: <each that is(has)>, <that is(has)>, <each who is(has)>, <who is(has)>, <each which is(has)> or <which is(has)> or alternatively <each of>, <of>, <each with> or <with>. The word <each> is needed if the <subject> or <object> is plural e.g., <Two cats each that is fierce etc.>.
A cat that is fierce, which has sharp claws, with a temper has a toy.

3.3 Every <Form 2> <subsidiary clause> begins with one of: <each that 'subject' is(has)>, <that 'subject' is(has)>, <each who 'subject' is(has)>, <who 'subject' is(has)>, <each which 'subject' is(has)> or <which 'subject' is(has)>. In the example, the <'subject'> is <the fierce cat>. Again,

the word <each> is needed if a plural is involved.
The toy which the fierce cat has is broken.

3.4 The possessive may be used to give the same result as in the previous example .i.e., <the fierce cat's toy> means the same as <the toy which the fierce cat has>.
The fierce cat's toy is mended.

3.5 The hyphen <-> acts in a similar way to the possessive, except that the order of possession is reversed i.e., <apple-pie> means the same as <the pie which has apple> and <control-room> means the same as <the room that has control>.
The apple-pie is delicious.

3.6 Let's look at <negation> in clauses using this.
There are two Scottie dogs, three Alsatian dogs and two Collie dogs.

3.7 And then this.
The second Scottie dog has a bone.

3.8 And then this. Note that we use <isnt> and not <isn't>.
Count each dog that isnt Scottie.
There are five dogs each that isnt Scottie.

3.9 And then this. Note again we use <hasnt> and not <hasn't>.
Count each Scottie dog that hasnt a bone.
There is just one Scottie dog that hasnt a bone.

3.10 Let's try a clause and ordinal example, starting with this.
Two ladies each has two more cats.

3.11 Followed by this.

Each cat has two more toys.

3.12 And finally this. Have a look at the <Mental Model> tab to verify the result.
The second toy of the first cat of the second lady is broken.

3.13 Here is an example of a preposition <inside>. The preposition here is treated as a feature of the <station>. Effectively, the <station> has an <inside> instance which the <train> then becomes a member of. Have a look at the <Mental Model> tab to see the treatment.
The train is inside the station.

3.14 Here is another example with the preposition <above>.
The plane is above the station.

3.15 And a final example with the preposition <beside>.
The station is beside the road.

Lesson 4 - General Verbs

4.1 Common verbs may be used, as shown. In the Mental Model the verb is changed to participle form: <Jack is swimming>. But <Jack swims> is <case perfect>, whilst <Jack is swimming> is <case imperfect>, with some difference in meaning, compensated for in the Model by means described later. Note that verbs must always be singular.
Jack swims.

4.2 In the Model, this is changed to: <Jack is climbing etc.>. The <climbing> is then regarded as a feature of <the hill> i.e., <the hill has climbing>, also thought of as <the climbing of the hill> e.g., <dog has biscuit> is similar to <biscuit of dog> i.e., we can regard <of> as an inversion of <has>.

Jack climbs the hill.

4.3 In the Mental Model, this represented as <Jack is jumping etc.>. The <instance> <jumping> is then represented as a feature of <the stream> i.e., <the stream has jumping>. The <instance> <across> is then treated as an adverb (effectively an adjective) of <jumping> to give <jumping is across>.
Jack jumps across the stream.

4.4 Plural <subjects> such as <two horses> use <each> to avoid the plural verb <run>.
Two horses each runs the race.

4.5 Verbs may have <direct objects> such a <the pail> and <indirect objects> such as <Jill>. In the Mental Model, this is represented as: <Jack is giving etc.>. Then <the pail has giving> i.e., <the giving of the pail>. Then <the giving is to>. Finally, <Jill has to>. The <to> is regarded as a sort of <in-box> for <Jill>.
Jack gives the pail to Jill.

4.6 This construction leads a model representing <reported speech>.
Check the <Mental Model> tab.
Jill thinks that Jack is selfish.

Lesson 5 - Verb Tenses

5.1 Verb tenses may be used, as exemplified. In the Model, the view is shifted to the verb tense and the present tense used. Effectively: <in the past, Jack is climbing the hill> The <view tense> <past/present/future> appears in the tab, with each <is/has> relation.
Jack climbed the hill.

5.2 <Each> is used to avoid the plural verb. Verb tense representations are typified by <swam/each swam> <(past)>, <swims/each swims> <(present)> and <will swim/each will swim> <(future)>.
Two men each will swim the Channel.

5.3 With the <is/has> verbs, tense representations are <was/has/each was/each had> <(past)>, <is/has/each is/each has> <(present)> and <will be/will have/each will be/each will have> <(future)>.
Jack will be very happy.

5.4 Verb tenses may be mixed in a sentence, with <won> in the <past> and <will receive> in the <future>. The tab shows how these are represented in the Model.
The girl who won the race will receive a prize.

Lesson 6 - Event Intervals

6.1 An <Event Interval> is an undefined period of time. Associated with it is an Ordering Integer which is shown in parentheses <[]> against each relation in the <Mental Model> tab. We begin by entering a sentence representing an action. The <Ordering Integer> is <0>.
Jack gets the pail.

6.2 We now enter another action sentence. This action is taking place at the same time as the previous action. This is shown by it having the same <Ordering Integer> of <0>.
Jill watches Jack.

6.3 The <Next> with optional comma, moves to the next event interval, shown by the Ordering Interval incrementing to <1>. The action <Jack climbs up the hill> happens in this new <Event Interval>. The previous actions of Jack and Jill are <case perfect> since they are of limited duration.

How <case imperfect> is dealt with is beyond the scope here.

Next, Jack climbs up the hill.

6.4 Since <Next> is not used, this action is taking place at the same time as the previous action and the <Ordering Integer> remains at <1>.

Jill carries the pail.

6.5 Since <Next> is used, a new Event Interval is implied, and the <Ordering Integer> steps on to <2>. There are separate <Ordering Integers> for <past>, <present> and <future> tenses.

Next, Jill gets the water.

6.6 The action takes place in the same <Event Interval> as the previous action.

Jack looks around.

6.7 The action takes place in a new <Event Interval>.

Next, Jack carries the pail.

6.8 The action takes place in the same <Event Interval> as the previous action.

Jill climbs down the hill.

Lesson 7 – Definitions

7.1 A definition begins with <Every> and mostly has a number of parts following <:>, each ending with <;> or <and> or both, or final full stop. The <Every> is mostly followed by an anonymous reference e.g., <person> and a clause e.g., <that is a doctor>.

Every person that is a doctor: has a medical degree; is caring; and is compassionate.

7.2 We can test the definition by saying <Jack> is an instance of a <doctor>.
Jack is a doctor.

7.3 And then asking for a description of Jack. <Describe> is <VERY SLOW>. Be patient. Look at the <Subvocalisation> tab to see Dialog thought processes.
Describe Jack.
There is just one Jack. Viewing Jack. Jack is a doctor, caring, and compassionate. Jack has a degree. Viewing the degree. The degree is medical. Leaving the degree. Leaving Jack.

7.4 Here we have nested an instance <is a quadruped> within the definition. We can now follow this by defining <quadruped>.
Every thing that is a cat: has a tail and whiskers; is crepuscular; and is a quadruped.

7.5 Like this.
Every thing that is a quadruped has a left, front leg, a right, front leg, a left, rear leg and a right, rear leg.

7.6 We can test the definition by saying <Felix> is an instance of a <cat>.
Felix is a cat.

7.7 And then asking for a description of Felix. <Describe> is <VERY SLOW>. Be patient. Look at the <Subvocalisation> tab to see Dialog thought processes.
Describe Felix.
There is just one Felix. Viewing Felix. Felix is a cat, crepuscular, and a quadruped. Felix has a tail, whiskers, a first leg, a second leg, a third leg, and a fourth leg. Viewing the first leg. The leg is left, and front. Leaving the first leg. Viewing the second leg. The leg is right, and front. Leaving the second leg. Viewing the third leg. The leg is left, and rear. Leaving the third leg. Viewing the fourth leg. The leg is right, and rear.

Leaving the fourth leg. Leaving Felix.

Lesson 8 – Views

8.1 We need to add some data.
A control-centre has two control-rooms.

8.2 Then add some more data.
The first room is main.

8.3 Then add some more data.
The second room is standby.

8.4 Now we can shift attention to the <first> <room> only by using <Viewing ...>.
Viewing the first room.

8.5 We now only need to say <room> not <first> or <second> <room>.
The room has a supervisory desk and an incident desk.

8.6 Now we can view the <supervisory desk> only using <Viewing ...> again.
Viewing the supervisory desk.

8.7 Again, we now only need to say <desk>.
The desk has a telephone and two screens.

8.8 However, we can still refer to an earlier topic e.g., <centre> if it can be unambiguously identified.
The centre has air conditioning.

8.9 We can go back a step like this.
Leaving the supervisory desk.

8.10 Or go back a further step like this. Or at any time we

can dismiss all views and view globally using <Viewing the whole>.

Leaving the previous.

Lesson 9 - Count, List & Describe

9.1 This and the following sentences illustrate <Count>. Start by adding some data.

A man has two Scottie dogs, three Alsatian dogs and a worried cat.

9.2 Now add some more.

Each Scottie dog has two toys and one biscuit.

9.3 And yet more.

Each Alsatian dog has one more toy and two more biscuits.

9.4 And even more.

The cat has one more biscuit and one more toy.

9.5 This is what we can now do using <Count>.

Count each man, each dog, each cat, each toy, and each biscuit.
There is just one man, five dogs, one cat, eight toys, and nine biscuits.

9.6 The following sentences illustrate <List>. Start by adding some data.

Mary, BoPeep, Aurora and Jill each likes Jack.

9.7 Now add some more.

Jack likes Mary, BoPeep and Jill.

9.8 Now try <List>. The word <person> is an anonymous reference, along with <thing> or any of <b-z> or <B-Z>.

List each person that likes Jack.
There is: Mary that is liking Jack; BoPeep that is liking Jack; Aurora that is liking Jack; and Jill that is liking Jack.

9.9 Now try <List> again.
List each person that Jack likes.
There is: Mary that Jack is liking; BoPeep that Jack is liking; and Jill that Jack is liking.

9.10 And something a bit more complicated using <List>.
List each person that Jack likes, that likes Jack.
There is: Mary that Jack is liking, that is liking Jack; BoPeep that Jack is liking, that is liking Jack; and Jill that Jack is liking, that is liking Jack.

9.11 The following sentence illustrate <Describe>. Start by adding some more data about <Humpty>.
Humpty sits on a wall.

9.12 And then yet more data about <Humpty>.
Humpty falls off the wall.

9.13 <Describe> is <VERY SLOW>. Be patient. The <Describe> algorithm is not very sophisticated, so the response tends to be naive. Select the <Subvocalisation> tab to see Dialog's thought processes.
Describe Humpty.
There is just one Humpty. Viewing Humpty. Humpty is sitting on a wall, and falling off a wall. Leaving Humpty.

Lesson 10 - Interface Controls

10.1 A suitable folder & name must be chosen for the file. The file is a text file <.TXT>. Nothing can be done until a new or existing file is referenced. Any current Dialog file is automatically saved. The file name is shown at the head of the <Dialog Box>.
The pushbutton that is 'New' creates a new file.

10.2 The file is a text file <.TXT>. Nothing can be done

until a new or existing file is referenced. Any current Dialog file is automatically saved. The file name is shown at the head of the <Dialog Box>.

The pushbutton that is 'Open' opens an existing file.

10.3   The sentence may be cleared or recalled using the <Clear/Previous> pushbutton.

The 'Sentence Box' receives a new sentence.

10.4 If the sentence is valid it appears in the <Dialog Box>. Otherwise, an error is reported in the <Sentence Box> & the <Enter> pushbutton changes to <Got it>. This must be clicked to accept the error. The sentence may then be edited to correct the error & <Enter> clicked.

The pushbutton that is 'Enter' enters the new sentence.

10.5 We are in that mode now. The <Tutorial> pushbutton changes to <Quit Tutorial>. If this is clicked, tutorial mode is ended. If tutorial mode is entered, any current Dialog file is automatically saved. The tutorial section is shown at the head of the <Dialog Box>.

The pushbutton that is 'Tutorial' enters a tutorial mode.

10.6 <Voice> is output only. This version does not support voice input.

The pushbutton that is 'Voice On' enables voice output.

10.7 Any current Dialog file is automatically saved.

The pushbutton that is 'Exit' ends the application.

APPENDIX B – AI DIALOG LESSONS

(This page is intentionally blank)

REFERENCES

Arnauld, A., & Lancelot, C. (1753 translation). CHAP IX.
Of the pronoun called relative. In A. Arnauld, & C.
Lancelot, *A general and rational grammar* (pp. 64-65).
London: J. Nourse.

Austen, J. (2003). Chapter I. In J. Austen, *Pride and Prejudice*
(p. 5). London: Penguin Books Ltd.

Butterfield, J. (2015). *Fowler's Dictionary of Modern English
Usage*. Oxford: Oxford University Press.

Cantor, G. (1895). Beiträge zur Begründung der transfiniten
Mengenlehre. *Math. Ann. 46*, 481-512.

Coleridge, S. T. (1983). Kubla Khan. In A. W. Allison, H.
Barrows, C. R. Blake, A. J. Carr, A. M. Eastman, &
H. M. English, *The Norton Anthology of Poetry, Third
Edition* (pp. 564-565). New York: W. W. Norton &
Company.

Cryan, D., Shatil, S., & Mayblin, B. (2013). Russell's System.
In D. Cryan, S. Shatil, & B. Mayblin, *Introducing
Logic* (pp. 26-27). London: Icon Books Ltd.

Cryan, D., Shatil, S., & Mayblin, B. (2013). The Syllogism. In D. Cryan, S. Shatil, & B. Mayblin, *Introducing Logic* (p. 6). London: Icon Books Ltd.

Cryan, D., Shatil, S., & Mayblin, B. (2013). Turing's recipe for AI. In D. Cryan, S. Shatil, & B. Mayblin, *Introducing Logic* (p. 64). London: Icon Books Ltd.

Curtiz, M. (Director). (1942). *Casablanca* [Motion Picture].

Fowler, H. D., & Fowler, F. (1989). *The Concise Oxford Dictionary Of Current English*. Oxford: Oxford University Press.

Garnham, A. (1994). The introduction of new referents into a model & Interpreting definite noun phrases. In A. Garnham, *Psycholinguistics Central Topics* (pp. 150-151). London: Routledge.

Goodrich, M. T., & Tamassia, R. (2015). Section 13.1: Graph terminology and representations. In M. T. Goodrich, & R. Tamassia, *Algorithm Design and Applications, Wiley, pp. 355–364* (pp. 355–364). New York: J. Wiley and Sons.

Hendrix, G. G. (1975). Expanding the utility of semantic networks through partitioning. *IJCAI'75 Proceedings of the 4th international joint conference on Artificial intelligence - Volume 1* (pp. 115-121). San Francisco, CA, USA: Morgan Kaufmann Publishers Inc.

Hofweber, T. (2018). Logic and Ontology. In E. N. Zalta, *The Stanford Encyclopedia of Philosophy*. Stanford: The Metaphysics Research Lab, Center for the Study of Language and Information,Stanford University.

Kempis, T. a. (2023). *The Imitation Of Christ.* London: Moncreiffe Press.

Kernighan, B. W., & Ritchie, D. M. (1988). A 11. Scope and Linkage. In B. W. Kernighan, & D. M. Ritchie, *The C Programming Language* (pp. 227-228). Englewood Cliffs, New Jersey: Prentice Hall P T R.

Lehman, F. (1992). Semantic Networks. *Computers & Mathematics with Applications*, Vol. 23, No. 2-5, 1-50.

Liberty, J. (2005). 4. Classes and Objects. In J. Liberty, *Programming C#* (pp. 67-103). Sebastopol, CA: O'Reilly Media Inc.

Lyon, G. (1974, January 1). Syntax-directed least-errors analysis for context-free languages: a practical approach. *Communications of the ACM Volume 17 Number 1*, pp. 3-14.

McGrath, M. (2020). Introducing SQL. In M. McGrath, *SQL in easy steps* (pp. 8-20). Leamington Spa: In Easy Steps Limited.

Seely, J. (2004). Countable and uncountable nouns. In J. Seely, *Oxford A-Z of Grammar & Punctuation* (p. 47). Oxford: Oxford University Press.

Seely, J. (2004). Indirect object. In J. Seely, *Oxford A-Z of Grammar & Punctuation* (p. 74). Oxford: Oxford University Press.

Seely, J. (2004). Passive voice. In J. Seely, *Oxford A-Z of Grammar & Punctuation* (pp. 110-111). Oxford: Oxford University Press.

Sowa, J. F. (1992). Semantic Networks, 1. Definitional Networks. In S. C. Shapiro, *Encyclopedia of Artificial Intelligence* (pp. 1494-1496). New York: J. Wiley and Sons.

Subramyam, M. (2005). 2.10 Switching Functions, 2.11 Sum-Of-Products (SOP) Form, 2.12 Product-Of-Sums (POS) Form, 2.13 Cannonical Forms. In M. Subramanyam, *Switching Theory And Logic Design* (pp. 118-131). New Delhi: Firewall Media.

Walmsley, M. (1997). 3.3 References. In M. Walmsley, *Programming in C++* (p. 29). London: Bernard Babani (publishing) Ltd.

Wegner, P. (1987). Dimensions of Object-Based Language Design. *Proceedings of OOPSLA '87* (pp. 168-182). New York, NY, USA: ACM.

Whitehead, A. N., & Russell, B. (2019). *Principia Mathematica*. Eastford CT, USA: Martino Fine Books.

Wikipedia. (2021, November 2). *Political views of Samuel Johnson*. Retrieved from Wikipedia: https://en.wikipedia.org/wiki/Political_views_of_Samuel_Johnson

Wikipedia. (2023, March 15). *Constituent (linguistics)*. Retrieved from Wikipedia: https://en.wikipedia.org/wiki/Constituent_(linguistics)

Wikipedia. (2023, March 15). *Dependency grammar*. Retrieved from Wikipedia: https://en.wikipedia.org/wiki/Dependency_grammar

Wikipedia. (2023, February 1). *Subgraph isomorphism problem*. Retrieved from Wikipedia: https://en.wikipedia.org/wiki/Subgraph_isomorphism_problem

ABOUT THE AUTHOR

Francis R. Belch is a former industrial computer system guru. He originated the control language for Britain's first computerised power station at Fawley in Hampshire, widely reported in the national press. He contributed to the design of the control system for the Zurich water supply network. He was associated with the training simulator for the European Spacelab. He was involved with the development of colour radar displays, on which he held British patents, and which were deployed, in the Oceanic Air Traffic Control Centre at Manchester, and at other UK and overseas airports, and featured in a popular BBC science TV programme. He contributed to the design of electricity distribution network control and monitoring systems for UK power utilities supplying the East Midlands, Midlands, and North-Western regions. He contributed to train tracking systems for the London Underground Central and Waterloo & City Lines. He acted as consultant on the power distribution control system for Eurotunnel. He has published a number of papers on these topics. For the past several years he has been deeply involved with blue sky research into so-called strong artificial intelligence (AI), now called artificial general intelligence (AGI). He is married with two children and lives in the UK.